A Call
to
Christian Patriotism

A Weekly Devotional Essay Series

HOWARD A. EYRICH

A Call to Christian Patriotism
A Weekly Devotional Essay Series
Howard A. Eyrich

Cover design by Melanie Schmidt

ISBN 978-1-885904-95-9

PRINTED IN THE UNITED STATES OF AMERICA
BY FOCUS PUBLISHING
Bemidji, Minnesota

"In a day marked by increasing secularism, cynicism, and concern by Christians over this state of affairs in our nation, we need to have a renewed understanding of a call to Christian patriotism. Howard Eyrich, an experienced minister and counselor, has brought his thoughts and convictions together in this new book, *A Call to Christian Patriotism*. The book leads believers to consider what Eyrich calls a 'Christian philosophy of patriotism.' The book is solidly biblical, warmly devotional, and spiritually enriching. I believe it comes at a needed time and I am happy to commend it wholeheartedly."

    Michael Milton, Ph.D.
    Chancellor & CEO
    Reformed Theological Seminary

"Dr. Eyrich's new book of devotionals about Christian patriotism is biblically based, theologically insightful and absolutely incredible! Don't miss these heart-moving and soul-stirring challenges. Every American needs to read this book."

    Dr. Ed Hindson
    Distinguished Professor
    Liberty University, VA

"Well done! Absolutely needed! I think we should get it into the hands of as many young people as possible."

    Hugh Jacks
    Retired President of Bell South Services and Motivational Speaker

"Dr. Howard Eyrich—pastor, professor, biblical counselor, and Christian patriot—has penned a very unique book. While it is a thought-provoking and soul-stretching 52-week devotional, it is much more than that. It is a practical theology of Christian engagement as a citizen of America and as a citizen of heaven. This book is for all those who desire a loving action plan for how Christians can impact their world for the cause of Christ."

    Dr. Bob Kellemen
    Executive Director of the Biblical Counseling Coalition
    Author of *Equipping Counselors for Your Church*

"Finally a book that gives the marriage of faith and freedom the attention it deserves! Every sincere believer in Jesus Christ has a freedom that transcends time and national borders but no one enjoys more freedom on earth than citizens of the USA. Though our freedom is a priceless gift, every patriot should feel a sense of obligation to do something worthy of the gift of freedom our forefathers purchased for us. I recommend every committed Christian read this book and follow the suggested Action Steps."

Jeff Struecker, Chaplain, U.S. Army Rangers
Major Struecker is a highly decorated combat veteran of "Black Hawk Down" movie and book fame. He is a pastor, husband, and father of five, Bronze Star, and Best Ranger Award.

"This book is timely, on target, and will be a blessing to many. We certainly need a good dose of Christian patriotism in America. This work could actually start a 'Christian Patriotism' movement!"

Charles Dunahoo
Coordinator of Christian Education and Publications
Presbyterian Church in America

A Call
to
Christian Patriotism

A Weekly Devotional Essay Series

Dedication

There are three groups of people to whom I would like to dedicate this work. I shall not name individuals.

First, this work is dedicated to our Colonial forefathers who gave both their lives and their fortunes to birth this nation. They, and the wives who stood behind them, were people with *feet of clay* just like each of us. Yet they were unique individuals whom God providentially brought together to give us a government "of the people, by the people and for the people" as one nation under God. I am grateful that they gave me the opportunity to be an American.

Second, this work is dedicated to the educators who, following my conversion, developed in me a love for learning. The faculty of Bob Jones University took the rather poor raw material I brought to their classes and prepared me for seminary. The professors at Faith Theological Seminary were patient and accepting, and constructively utilized my constant arguing to benefit me and my fellow students. Several faculty members at Dallas Theological Seminary encouraged me to be creative in ministry. The faculty of the Christian Counseling and Educational Foundation were critical in mentoring me into the practical application of Scripture to the business of living christianly.

Third, this work is dedicated to the seven "generals" under whom I have served in the Lord's army. These men have inspired me by their vision, critiqued me with a desire to perfect me, and encouraged me to use my God-given gifts to serve God and country. Their leadership has been invaluable in providing me the opportunity to develop leaders.

Appreciation

A book may be the idea of an individual. A book may be the product of tenacious hard work on behalf of the author. But, a book is never the product of the author alone. There are several people who have enabled me to bring this project to fruition.

Over the past year, I began to write and send my devotional essays to my administrative assistant to read in her spare time, asking her to give me feedback. Her response was extraordinarily positive, and she continued to push me forward. In addition to being a highly capable office administrator, Sharon Penn is a gifted artist. I told her that I wanted her to paint an original picture that would portray a Christian patriot theme in a more abstract than concrete manner. She agreed, and a copy of her painting is included below.

My wife, Pam, not only patiently endured the process, but also provided the early editorial assistance.

Leigh Ann Reese helped with the technical task of formatting the text so I could present it to others for evaluation.

Last, but most certainly not least, Ike Reeder has been indispensible with editing. His suggestions for the ordering of the devotional essays and the transitional phrasing were most helpful. He also helped me refine the title of *A Call to Christian Patriotism,* and in the process provided a missing dimension in my original thinking.

Sharon Penn

Table of Contents

Preface

Preface

Why a Book on Christian Patriotism?

Over the past year, the impetus for this book has grown in my heart in two ways. First, it has grown out of my own personal devotional life. At the same time, however, I was experiencing great agony over the turmoil that has burdened my country. I love my God and I love my country. One morning the thought occurred to me that a devotional guide that focused on what it means to be a Christian while at the same time, historically, looking at what it means to be a Patriot could spawn life application in the form of an action plan. This type of devotional might well be used of God to inspire many Christians to embrace the important responsibility of citizenship. To be an American is exhilarating! To be a Christian Patriot is humbling. To serve the Lord and glorify Him through the writing of this book is a privilege. To God be the glory!

My own personal journey as a Christian Patriot began with being born on Lincoln's birthday and with my mother naming me after him—my middle name is Abraham. In her simple way, with her limited educational background, she taught me the basics of American history through the lens of being a Christian. However, like most teenagers, during my high school years I questioned what two-hundred-year-old documents had to do with life in our modern world. Their inherent relevance escaped me. In fact, the whole idea of studying history seemed to be a boring waste of time. It was not until after my conversion at the beginning of my senior year in high school that history began to interest me. Over time, I realized that a committed Christian is a thinking and active Christian. Thus, my understanding of my position in the church and in my country began to grow, as did my *philosophy* of being a churchman and a Christian.

A Philosophy of Christian Patriotism

Many of us, though, do not think of ourselves as *philosophers*. That word itself is a frightening one, conjuring up images of stodgy professors, Greeks clad in togas, and argumentative rhetoricians. As I embarked on this project, however, it began to dawn on me that I was working out a *philosophy* of what it means to be a Christian Patriot. Not a philosophy in the sense above, but rather an understanding of what is the core of my beliefs as a Christian and as a Patriot. What were my bedrock principles? I am, at this juncture, tempted to delineate that philosophy for you, the reader; but educational pedagogy generated a resistance to this course of action. During this year it is my desire that *you* will be intentionally pondering the question: "What does it mean to be a Christian Patriot?" Rather than tell you my philosophy of Christian Patriotism here, I will let you discover it throughout these weekly readings, as I discovered it in writing them.

For example, in my profession I have been, among other things, a professor at several seminaries in southeast America. Over the years of my work I have developed a philosophy of Christian Education. These are the core beliefs concerning education that I, as a Christian, believe are absolutely necessary, not only for right education to occur, but for that education to be practiced by Christians and in a Christlike manner. The components of that philosophy include:

1. The content of Christian Education is defined by the Bible.
2. The ability of the recipient to benefit from Christian Education is dependent on the individual having a personal relationship with Jesus Christ.
3. Educational methodology must be adapted to the listener.
4. Prayer is essential for both the student and the teacher.

Thus, I can state my philosophy of Christian Education. As a Christian educator I am committed to communicating the content of the Bible through prayerful preparation by teacher and student and careful assessment of, and adaptation to, student learning styles. As we continue this journey toward Christian Patriotism together this year, use this as a model to grapple with your own philosophy of Christian Patriotism. What does it mean to you that you are a citizen of America and, in an even greater way, also a citizen of heaven? How should we act differently than those around us who do not believe the same as we do? These questions are vital and will arise throughout the year.

A Passion for Christian Patriotism
As I mentioned earlier, it is important to remember that a thinking Christian is an active and passionate Christian. One of the unique things about this book is that it not only encourages you to think about Christian Patriotism, but also engages you in expanding your active role in citizenship. As you read, develop your philosophy of Christian Patriotism, but don't stop there. You should also develop your passion for citizenship.

There are only three things in life about which I become emotional, three things that consistently stir up my passions. One is Jesus, who hung on that cross to die for me. He died for me, the one who drove the nails into his hands; for while I was yet a sinner, Christ died for me. He redeemed me from the slave market of sin and gave me the gift of eternal life. The second is the family God has graciously given to me. While I do not deserve it in any way, He gave to me a Christian mother, Christian in-laws, two children and their spouses, and eight grandchildren who know Jesus as their personal savior. What a blessing to be surrounded by a family that loves the Lord! The third thing is my country, in which God privileged me to be born. This country, America, was founded on the core of Christianity and for so long has been a beacon in a world shrouded in the darkness of sin. The passion of this devotional book derives from these three wells of emotion. I trust that God will be pleased to well up in you a passion for Jesus, family, and country as you join me on this year-long journey. It is *your* philosophy that will give you direction. It is *your* passion that will give energy to your footsteps and spring into your gait.

How This Devotional Essay Works

This is not the typical devotional book on three counts. First, it is not a daily devotional guide; it is a weekly one. Second, it does not provide you with a "nugget to chew on for the day" for spiritual delight. Rather, it gives you a passage pregnant with principle that is to guide your thinking on citizenry for the week. Third, it does not end with the reading. The reading is the beginning of an action plan for the week.

You will best utilize this book first of all by setting aside 20 minutes or so on Monday morning to read the essay for that week. Monday is effectively the first day of the week. Engaging the essay will challenge you to be a Christian Patriot each Monday morning. Also, in God's kind providence, the passage will be relevant to you throughout the week as you encounter news, political decisions, and situations in your own life. As a supplement to your Scripture reading, I pray that God will use each Monday's reading to have a daily impact throughout the rest of the week.

Prayer

The process of using this book is not complicated, but it will take determined effort. Each week when you sit down to absorb the reading for that Monday, you should begin with this Prayer:

> Father, you have given me the privilege to become a child of God (John 1:12). You have also given me the privilege to be born in America. This devotional is going to challenge me to walk with you in the manner in which I walk as an American. As your testimony, your Gospel is at stake in the way I walk as a Christian, so also is the welfare of my country. Help me, Lord, to take the challenge today and determine how I can implement my actions this week so that I make a difference as did my forefathers. Amen.

The purpose of praying this prayer is twofold. The first, obviously, is to worship God and acknowledge your dependence on him. The second reason is principle: it is to accustom you to the idea that the quality of your walk with Jesus should frame the quality of your citizenship. The closer you walk with Jesus, the more capacity you have to be effective in your responsibilities as an American citizen. The apostle Paul makes it abundantly clear that Christians have civic responsibilities. Over this next year you will be refining your understanding and your capacity to execute these responsibilities with greater clarity.

I have provided a prayer at the end of each meditation to help you prayerfully focus upon the ideas discussed in the essay.

Devotional Reading

After prayer, it is time to read the devotional for Monday morning. The book is not dated so you can begin on the Monday immediately following your acquiring of this book and continue for 52 consecutive weeks. On the top right of the page is a place to write the date you read the passage. If you miss a week, simply pick the book up again the next week.

In the devotional there are two items to read. First, on the top, is the Scripture passage for the day. These passages are not random and have been chosen to directly relate to and correlate with the historical, biblical, and theological lesson espoused in the essay. Please take the time to read the biblical passage first, and then read the essay for the week.

Action Steps
Following the devotional essay there are two more steps.

1. Prayerfully contemplate what you have read. As you review the main thrust of the devotional, ask God to teach you how to implement it.
2. There is space provided for you to determine one to three action steps that you will engage during the week with a space for you to date when you have completed the action step.

This is followed with a place for you to record the outcome of your action. Sometimes there will be no immediate outcome. Below is an example of how this appears. In *Action Step I*, there will likely be no immediate response from the recipients for you to record. Here is an example of the action steps plan and some possible ideas for action:

Action Step 1   I will send an e-mail or letter to each of my congressmen and state legislators pledging my commitment to pray for them each Monday during the next year.

Date completed_____

Outcome_____

Action Step 2   I will call my mayor (or county commissioner or other local official) this week and make an appointment to treat him to lunch, explaining that I am taking up a new commitment to be involved in my civic responsibility.

Date completed_____

Outcome_____

Action Step 3   I will purchase a copy of this book to present to _____ and encourage him/her to take up this challenge.

Date completed _____

Outcome_____

On each Monday, at the end of the reading, you will be prompted to engage in one to three projects for the next week. You determine the project within your comfort zone, your time frame and your sphere of influence. It is imperative, however, that you put feet to your devotion. In the appendix of this book is a suggested list of action projects.

Welcome to the spirit of Christian Patriotism. In the process of working through this book I hope you will begin to develop a philosophy of Christian Patriotism and an action outlet for your passion.

Follow developments and find additional materials at: www.calltochristianpatriotism.com.

Watch for small group study guides. I am anticipating a ten week plan and a one year plan.

Howard Eyrich
James Hill Community,
Hoover, AL

Week 1   Date: _____
In the Beginning God
Text: *Genesis 1:1–24*

Weekly Reading:
In the beginning God created the world. Each step of creation was stamped with a golden tag that read, "God saw that it was good." We cannot even begin to imagine the wonder of Adam when God breathed the breath of life into him and he became a conscious being.

Some people deny that children are born with a sin nature; at least they deny it until they have to change that first diaper of a defiant infant who stiffens the legs in absolute resistance. From that point forward the child is in need of corrective discipline in order to become a reasonable human being. This was not the case with Adam. He awoke an adult, completely able *not* to sin. He awoke an adult, completely able to comprehend and appreciate the wonder before him. He awoke an adult, complete with the capacity to engage in regency over God's creation. This capacity is observed in the enormous responsibility assigned to him in the naming of the animals (Gen. 2:19). This same task demonstrates his capacity for self-awareness since this mission is strategically placed between God's conclusion that "It is not good for man to be alone . . ." and the creation of Eve.

The next chapter records the saddest event in human history: the fall of man. From this point forward God becomes the Holy Parent of a defiant and resistant creation. The natural condition of man is pictured in Romans 1. Natural man suppresses the revelation of God and chooses the rebellious path that eventuates in God turning him over to a reprobate mind (Rom. 1:28). The Old Testament is full of examples of God bringing both judgment and grace upon His people and on others around the Israelites. God tells Moses that Israel will take the Promised Land when the wickedness of the Amorites is full (Gen. 15:16). The great flood from which God delivered Noah and his family, the judgment of Sodom and Gomorrah, the demise of Egypt after 400 years, the cruel slavery of Israel, the discipline of Israel by pagan nations after refusing to hear the prophets' call for repentance— these are all records of God disciplining his creation, even his chosen people. In the New Testament, Jesus tells the parable of the vineyard that pictures the process and the slow realization of all who come to Him (Matt. 20:1–16). Immediately after that, he gives prophesy of His impending crucifixion.

Our Founding Fathers recognized this downward spiral of humanity and the principle of the *parenting* God of the Bible who, from time to time, instituted interventions resulting in revival and a fresh beginning. They also understood the necessity of corporate checks and balances to restrain this natural devolution. Probably the clearest expression of this is in the Preamble to the Declaration of Independence.

> *When in the course of human events, it becomes necessary for one people to dissolve the political bands which have connected them with another, and to assume among the powers of the earth, the separate and equal station to which the Laws of Nature and of Nature's God entitle them, a decent respect to the opinions of mankind requires that they should declare the causes which impel them to the separation. We hold these truths to be self-evident, that all men are created equal, that they are endowed by their Creator with certain inalienable rights that among these are life, liberty and the pursuit of happiness. That to secure these rights, governments are instituted among men, deriving their just powers from the consent of the governed. That whenever any form of government becomes destructive of these ends, it is the right of the people to alter or abolish it, and to institute new government, laying its foundation on such principles and organizing its powers in such form, as to them shall seem most likely to effect their safety and happiness.*

America exists, in its very infrastructure, on that primary principle of the Bible: mankind, left completely to pursue its own devices, inevitably devolves into wickedness, callousness, and rebellion against God. Government's responsibility, then, is to set up a secular system of checks and balances that help the church hold society accountable for sin (Rom. 13).

Prayer:
Almighty God, Creator, Sustainer, Judge and Redeemer, as Christian Patriots we offer our thanks today for our forefathers who took you and your Word seriously. We thank you that in your providence you led them to craft a set of documents that provided an opportunity for the preaching of the Gospel and the expansion of the Kingdom of God. But our hearts are fearful of judgment as we observe leaders and citizens who progressively engage in the Romans 1 spiral. Grant us, Lord God, revival, and let it begin with the "House of God."

Action Steps:

ACTION STEP 1

Date Completed _____
Outcome

ACTION STEP 2

Date Completed _____
Outcome

ACTION STEP 3

Date Completed _____
Outcome

Week 2   Date:_____
The Church: A Model for Our Nation
Text: *Acts 2:37–47, Revelation 2:1–7*

Weekly Reading:
Midway through the ministry of the apostle Paul, a situation arose at
Thessalonica that had the appearance of the social riots many of us have
observed on television newscasts in recent years (Acts 17:1–9). Embedded
in this record is an interesting comment by the perpetrators. As they are
dragging Jason before the city authorities they are shouting, "These men
who have upset the world have come here also." Within a generation
this fledgling church model had replicated itself with such frequency and
life-changing power that it generated a fear in pagan society of being
overwhelmed throughout the known world.

In our text for meditation today, we can discern five characteristics of
that early church that turned the world upside down. While the content of
these traits, with reference to the church, are filled with religious content,
the model provides a powerful pattern for our nation. These five traits are
teaching, fellowship, worship, service, and outreach. In the church the
content of teaching is biblical doctrine. Fellowship is the socialization of
believers around the person of Christ. Worship is the corporate offering
of praise, prayers, and personal commitment. Service is the giving of self
to the maintenance and extension of the work of God. Outreach, finally, is
extending the good word of the Gospel to the world.

From a Christian Patriot's perspective this model has the following
content: teaching is the formal and informal transference of the meaning
and intent of the Constitution and Bill of Rights in the context of their
historical development and the societal struggle to interpret and apply them.
Fellowship is the socialization of the populace around these documents
as the soul of our nation. Worship is the corporate recognition of God's
good hand upon America and the encouragement of one another through
the use of music, particularly anthems of independence that celebrate
American values (e.g., *"My Country, 'Tis of Thee," "America the Beautiful"*),
and other activities. Service ranges from voting to holding political office
and everything between. Outreach is the proclamation that America, while
not being a Christian entity or a perfect society in which ideals are realities,
is the land of freedom that welcomes the rest of the world who would
embrace the soul and ideation of our Constitution. As Christian Patriots, we
must practice *both*.

Our Founding Fathers drew liberally from the Bible in fashioning and developing a model for America. However, just like the church, America drifted from this model and developed into a bureaucratic institution. The Lord Jesus addresses this issue in his letter to the church at Ephesus in Revelation 2. In this letter He identifies the problem as "you have left your first love." He commends them for their work, their toil, and their perseverance; but for their diminished passion for Jesus He warns them that they are in danger of losing it all (the removal of their *lampstand* v. 5). He then instructs this church regarding the remedy for the situation. He tells them to remember what they have lost, to repent and to return to the deeds "that you did at first."

This prescription fits for America also. We must develop a personal and corporate memory of what we were given. We must personally and corporately repent for our drifting. We must return to the deeds of our Founding Fathers, the rehearsing of, and the application of, the Constitution and Bill of Rights. This process begins with the individual Christian Patriot. We must rehearse thanksgiving and prayer as did our forefathers. We must repent for our loss of passion for Christ and the implication for Christian living in the public arena. We must return to the deeds that characterized our beginning.

Prayer:
Father, giver of all good gifts, we remember today the gifts that you have given to us both in the structural establishment of this nation and the models of the deeds of our forefathers. Grant us, Lord, good memories; grant us repentance for drifting as Christians and Americans; and grant us the capacity to rejuvenate the models given to us in the early church and in our American forefathers. Help me, Lord, today and this week to take action! Amen.

Action Steps:

ACTION STEP 1

Date Completed _____
Outcome

ACTION STEP 2

Date Completed _____
Outcome

ACTION STEP 3

Date Completed _____
Outcome

Week 3   Date: _____
A Call to Responsible Citizenship
Text: *Joshua 7*

Weekly Reading:
Whether you look at Judaism or Christianity you will find that there is a consistent intertwining of the individual and the corporate. The ten spies who did not believe were spokesmen for the nation. Their personal unbelief led a groundswell of corporate unbelief that overshadowed those who did believe God. As a result the whole generation was disciplined by God. Yet the individual faith and belief of a few men, generations later, so impacted both the nation of Israel and the pagan kingdom in which they lived that pagan kings were converted to God and actually financed the return of Israel to the land (see Daniel, Ezra, and Nehemiah).

This week's reading is a record of a reality that moderns find difficult to swallow (Joshua 7:24–26). It is beyond the scope of our purpose here to discuss the frightening and horrifying event of Achan and his family's downfall. It shall have to suffice to refer you to Deuteronomy 29:29 and Romans 11:33. However, there are principles in today's passage that impinge upon our national life as Christians.

First, we should note that the consequences of individual sin bring the tarnishing of God's glory. Achan's sin caused God to allow Joshua's army to be routed, and in the process the glory of God was impacted (v.9). This individual sin also impacted the community, according to verse 5, which tells us "the hearts of the people melted and became as water." Individual sin impacts one's relationship with God (v. 20). Furthermore, Achan's individual sin impacted his family. His whole family was executed because of his covetousness (v. 24–25).

Second, there is corporate responsibility for individual sin. God says to Joshua, "Israel has sinned and they have transgressed My covenant . . ." (v. 11). Within the church and within a nation we are responsible to hold each other accountable to live righteously. When one sins, the corporate body of the church is impacted as is the corporate body of the nation. In this case there were two immediate effects on the nation. They suffered a military loss and they had to participate in the execution of the guilty. Examples in our own time include Germany during the first half of the twentieth century. The German people bore a corporate responsibility for Hitler's individual sins (and the many that willingly followed him). Germany, the cradle of the Reformation, strayed so far from its Christian heritage as to allow the likes of Hitler to subvert the political structure. Providence, through the allies (many of whom individually lived with the horrific memory of executing that justice), visited the consequences upon their evil.

God providentially gave America a foundation that is largely consistent with righteousness. No, God did not directly make a covenant with America, but our Founding Fathers gave us a framework that recognized God's providence and set forth a pattern of freedom, justice, and mercy that honored God. When we as individuals sin, we detract from God's glory. We disregard his providential hand in our nation. As Christians we disregard his redemptive work in Jesus Christ. As a consequence we bring judgment on our nation; we weaken its fabric. We bring disgrace to the Kingdom of God because in our sin we look no different than the unbeliever.

There is one more lesson for us in this passage. The corporate community is responsible for justice (v. 24–26). As Christian Patriots, this justice must always begin with repentance (v. 6–9). The community must recognize the sin (v. 12) and investigate it (v. 13–25). The community must take responsibility for discipline (v. 24–26). God has given us this responsibility both as citizens of His church and as citizens of America. In the process His blessings are restored.

Prayer:
O, God of providence, who has blessed us through the redemptive work of Christ so that we are new creations, enable us to recognize the temptation of sin and to choose not to engage it. Help us to exercise our Kingdom citizenship in the manner in which we conduct our temporal citizenship. Help us as churchmen and patriots to take corporate responsibility for mutual accountability and justice.

Action Steps:

ACTION STEP 1

Date Completed _____
Outcome

ACTION STEP 2

Date Completed _____
Outcome

ACTION STEP 3

Date Completed _____
Outcome

Week 4   Date: _____
So Why Be a Christian Patriot?
Text: *Exodus 8:20–27*

Weekly Reading:
So far, we have examined the nature of America in relationship to its Christian heritage and our responsibilities as Christians who live in a country whose government was framed by Judeo-Christian ethics and principles. But the question remains: "Why be a Christian Patriot?"

John Blanchard, the British apologist and theologian, cites a World Evangelical Alliance Religious Commission study regarding the worldwide problem of persecution.[1] According to this organization, more than 200 million people from more than 60 countries are denied basic human rights in some fashion simply because they are Christians. While there have been small pockets of official persecution or the circumscription of human rights during the course of American history, this is not the norm. If you are looking for the answer to the question, "Why should I be a Christian Patriot?" it can be found here. The American Constitution and the Bill of Rights provide your protection. You can witness, preach, teach, and sing about your faith because these documents guarantee your freedom to do so. You can work to correct America's flaws.

Religious freedom in America, however, is under attack. The attack is occasionally direct, but most of the time it is subtle. Some of the direct hits have come in the form of legalized abortion and the censure of school prayer. Some of the more indirect attacks have come in individual censures such as student speeches or prayer at athletic events. More recently there has been developing a broader societal remonstration for Christians to keep their religion inside their homes and houses of worship. In other words, religious freedom does not include the public application of a Christian worldview.

Our passage for today records a perspective regarding our worship that, because of our heritage of religious freedom, we often forget. After experiencing several plagues, Pharaoh exasperatedly exclaims, "Go, and sacrifice to your God within the land!" This is not what Moses requested and he refuses to accept this offer. Here is the reason he gives to Pharaoh. "It is not right to do so, for if we shall sacrifice to the Lord our God what is an abomination to the Egyptians before their eyes, will they not then stone

---
[1]   John Blanchard, *Jesus: Dead or Alive?* (New York: EP Books, Inc.) 8.

us?" (Exodus 8:25–27). There is a truth embedded in this scene that explains why people are hostile to Christians. This truth is the fact that the nature of the Israelites' worship would be totally unacceptable to the Egyptians. That same truth is evident in our worship today.

Our worship is a display of beliefs that the world despises. Our worship begins with the recognition that God is the Creator—with this, we have just isolated most of the hard sciences. Our worship acknowledges that we are sinners and enemies of God—we have just isolated the social sciences. Our worship exclusively embraces a resurrected Jesus—we have just isolated all other religions. Our worship proclaims that Jesus is coming again as the Righteous King—we have just isolated all other political systems. Our worship is an abomination to the world. Our Founding Fathers understood this reality. To secure our liberty they set forth a structure that, on one hand, did not allow the government to establish religion and, on the other hand, guaranteed free expression to religion.

So, again, let's ask the question, "Why be a Christian Patriot?" The answer should be self-evident. It takes a passionate vigilance to maintain religious freedom in a culture that is rapidly embracing paganism. We cannot afford to be patriots who simply want to retain a way of life. Neither can we afford to be Christians who naively enjoy liberty. We must be Christians who are completely involved in the propagation of the Gospel, while at the same time taking the responsibility to be Americans, so as to preserve our freedom for the sake of the Gospel: thus we are Christian Patriots.

Prayer:
O, Lord God, maker of heaven and earth. In the name of the resurrected Jesus we come to you today. We come with grateful hearts for the freedom from sin secured by Jesus on the cross. We come with grateful hearts for the freedom you secured for us as Christians in the establishment of this nation. Now, Father, enable us to be obedient Christians who freely share the Gospel and enable us the determination to enter into the self-governing responsibility bestowed upon us so as to guard the gift of freedom which you have granted.

Action Steps:

ACTION STEP 1

Date Completed _____
Outcome

ACTION STEP 2

Date Completed _____
Outcome

ACTION STEP 3

Date Completed _____
Outcome

Week 5   Date: _____
The "Christian" in Christian Patriot
Text: *Acts 2:42–43; 4:32–37; 8:1–4*

Weekly Reading:
The *Patriot* in Christian Patriot is rather clearly focused on the love of country and one's service to it. What, however, is that *Christian* to be focused upon? The Christian Patriot must be engaged in the expansion of the Kingdom of God. The only real hope of the Christian Patriot is the expansion of the Kingdom of God. It is only as the church is strengthened, expanded, and permeating America can we hope to experience the integrity of the intent of our Founding Fathers. Patriots are not primarily about preserving America. That is, it is not our main purpose to preserve our nation. Preserving our nation is a consequence of the impact of the Gospel, just as the turning of the world upside down was a consequence of preaching the Gospel.

So, how does the Christian Patriot advance the Kingdom of God? The passages cited for our meditation today indicate the four activities of the early church that we must emulate to accomplish this goal that is the focus the Lord laid out for his followers in Matthew 28:18–20.

The first activity is PRAYER that is characterized by thanksgiving and expectation. The apostle Paul sums it up this way, "Continue steadfastly in prayer, being watchful (expectant) in it with thanksgiving. At the same time, pray also for us, that God may open to us a door for the Word, to declare the mystery of Christ. . ." (Col. 4:2–3).

PREACHING with content and power is the second activity. Peter's sermons in Acts 2 and 3 are full of content and power. He reviews the history of Israel as culminating in the crucifixion of Jesus and the culpability of the Jews ("this Jesus whom you crucified"). The power is seen in his call for repentance and the conversion of three thousand souls (2:41).

The third activity is pointed deeds of JUSTICE and MERCY. On the one side is the concern for people's physical suffering and the ministry of healing. On the other side is the ministry of caring for their material needs (Acts 4:32–37). When you look across the American landscape, hospital after hospital has the imprint of Christ's church. The church taught society the meaning of the ministry of mercy and justice, as observed, for example, in the largest such ministry in the world—the Salvation Army.

The last activity is that of personal EVANGELISM. Evangelism can and should be done when the church is gathered for worship, but this is not where the power of transforming a society is unleashed. The church's power is unleashed when the church is scattered. Luke says it this way: "they were scattered throughout the regions of Judea and Samaria . . . . Now those who were scattered went about preaching the word" (Acts 8:2, 4). Just imagine if every member of an evangelical church preached the Gospel and led one soul to Christ and into a local church this year. In just one year the church would double in size. If this continued for just five years, you can do the math and see where the church would be!

So, it must be concluded that the *Christian* in Christian Patriot is Kingdom-centered. Christian Patriots practice these four activities and contribute to the expansion of the Kingdom of God. As a consequence, the American nation is strengthened.

Prayer:
Father, I repent of my desire to be an American first and a Christian second. I repent for being more concerned for America than I am for the Kingdom of God. I repent for not practicing these four primary activities as a citizen of the Kingdom of God. But, Father, I thank you that as I am obedient to you my obedience benefits my nation indirectly. Lord, bless me by enabling me to be obedient. And, Lord—God bless America.

Action Steps:

ACTION STEP 1

Date Completed _____
Outcome

ACTION STEP 2

Date Completed _____
Outcome

ACTION STEP 3

Date Completed _____
Outcome

Week 6   Date: _____
The God of This World and the Christian Patriot
Text: *Romans 6–9*

Weekly Reading:
Would it be possible today to forge a great nation with a form of government where human beings are, at least in principle, individually valued and where an ethical sense of right and wrong is dominant? Our forefathers were not flawless individuals, but they were at the forefront of their time in bringing about a form of government superior to any that existed previously. They drew in part on their readings of great writers such as John Locke and ancient Greek philosophers. Without doubt, the majority of the Founding Fathers were Christians, along with a good sprinkling of Deists (who gave credence to the values and ethical framework of Christianity). Certainly the principles and standards we hold dear color how we think, behave, relate to others, and conduct business; so it was for them. The Judeo-Christian influence was at the core of society. Regarding slavery and women's rights, we can only wish our forefathers had understood what we over time and with great struggle and debate have come to understand. However, despite their flaws, our forefathers provided us with an enduring foundation from which we could fight and set into law the correctives of contemporary society.

As Christian Patriots we must always keep a full theological perspective in mind. This begins with the sovereignty of God. While we sometimes struggle to conceptualize this in the midst of great human tragedies—like the earthquake and tsunami in Japan and the tornados in Alabama (2011), or the awful wars of modern history—the Scripture declares God's sovereignty everywhere. The apostle Paul informs us that Satan is the god of this world (system). The phrase "god of this world" (2 Cor. 4:4; Eph. 2:2; John 12:31) indicates that Satan is the major influence on the mind-set expressed by the ideals, opinions, goals, hopes and views of the majority of people. Therefore cultures express his influence through ideas, speculations, and false religions. His major tool appears to be deception (John 8:44). These two realities are brought together at the cross. Here God the Son announces "It is finished!" Redemption was accomplished. Henceforth that redemption is being applied until Jesus returns to effect the final application of the judgment of Satan and his angels.

As Patriots who are Christians, our hope rests in that finished work of Jesus to effect the redemption of our souls. As Christians who are Patriots we rest our national welfare in the hands of God through our Constitution and Bill of Rights. With these instruments God has put on us the responsibility to utilize the freedom to "form [the] more perfect Union" that they provide. If we, like ancient Israel, neglect our responsibilities, we will suffer eventual demise at our own hands as a result of our own neglect. We will sacrifice both our religious and political freedom on the altar of expediency. We will allow the very roots of our Judeo-Christian framework to be discarded. We will allow the god of the world to deceive us and our leaders to implement more and more concepts that will destroy the God-given gift of America.

Christian Patriots arise! Take up your responsibility to permeate our culture with the power of the Gospel! We are embattled in spiritual warfare, and only as we live the Gospel and speak its implications into our culture can we hope to defeat the "god of this world."

Prayer:
O, Redeemer Jesus, thank you that you finished the work of redemption on the cross. Thank you that we have the confidence that you are going to finally judge the god of this world and cast him into hell. But, Lord, in the meantime you have given us your Word so that we are not ignorant of his schemes. Now Lord, grant to us the power to proclaim the Gospel by word and life in every dimension of our lives!

Action Steps:

ACTION STEP 1

Date Completed _____
Outcome

ACTION STEP 2

Date Completed _____
Outcome

ACTION STEP 3

Date Completed _____
Outcome

Week 7   Date: _____
A Call to Return to Our Roots
Text: *2 Chronicles 7:14*

Weekly Reading:
To whom else could we best look for an understanding of the American experiment than the father of our nation, George Washington? Dr. Peter Lillback, in his seminal work on Washington's Christianity, *A Sacred Fire*, records a letter Washington wrote to a Hebrew congregation in Savannah:

> *May the same wonder-working Deity, who long since delivered the Hebrews from their Egyptian Oppressor and planted them in the promised land—whose Providential Agency has lately been conspicuous in establishing these United States as an independent Nation—still continue to water them with the dews of Heaven and to make the inhabitants of every denomination participate in the temporal and spiritual blessings of that people whose God is Jehovah.[2]*

When Israel departed Egypt, Moses records this commentary: "And a mixed multitude went up also with them; and flocks, herds, and very much cattle" (Ex. 12:38). An honest review of American history underscores the fact that a mixed multitude flowed from England and Europe into this land. However, a modern interpretation of our history, which plays down the importance of Christianity as the foundation upon which this nation is built, simply ignores the facts.

Our text for today characterizes the various streams of people who were the fountainhead of the philosophical concepts that birthed this nation. The popular picture of Washington kneeling and praying personifies the core of America. Furthermore, from the original charter of the Virginia Company—which stated the propagation of the Christian religion as a goal of the flourishing towns of New England in which faith, values, commerce, and education were rooted in a biblical framework—the humility and dependence on the God of our Founding Fathers is evident.

---

[2]   Sacred Fire p. 577-578

For example, the attitude of humility expressed in dependence on God can be found in the documents adopted by local governments of the Massachusetts Bay area. Typically they read after this manner:

> *We Covenant with the Lord and with one another and do bind ourselves in the presence of God, to walk together in all his ways, accordingly as he is pleased to reveal himself to us in his Blessed word of truth. And do more explicitly, in the name and fear of God, profess and protest to walk as followeth through the power and goodness of the Lord Jesus Christ.*[3]

"If my people who are called by my name will humble themselves . . ." is our challenge today. All of us who call on His name must humble ourselves and repent of our nation's spurning of the goodness of God in His great gifts of freedom by our neglecting to participate in the responsibilities of self-government and the utilization of our freedom effectively for the propagation of the Christian religion. In our repentance we must engage in the political process in at least three ways: educating ourselves and filtering what we learn through a biblical grid, conducting our lives in a godly fashion, and voting. In addition, in our repentance, we must be propagators of the Christian religion, both in evangelism and in justice and mercy.

Prayer:
Father, as your child living in a nation endowed with great freedom and responsibility, I express repentance for our sin as a people. We have failed by exchanging arrogance for humility. We have failed by exchanging licentiousness for freedom. We have failed by exchanging self-indulgence for worship. Father, we have sinned. Grant us repentance and forgiveness. Enable us to remember what we had and revive our passion for freedom and righteousness. Father, begin with me!

---

[3]   Gragg, 56

Action Steps:

ACTION STEP 1

Date Completed _____
Outcome

ACTION STEP 2

Date Completed _____
Outcome

ACTION STEP 3

Date Completed _____
Outcome

Week 8   Date: _____

What Is Truth? The Logical Law of Non-contradiction

Text: *John 18:28–38*

Weekly Passage:

Toward the end of Jesus' trial before Pilate, Pilate asks him, "So, you are a king?" Jesus' answer ends with the statement, "Everyone who is of truth hears My voice (John 18:37). Pilate's response to Jesus, "What is truth?" was likely not intended to be a philosophical question. It was much more likely a statement of sarcasm. Something like, "Oh, and what do you know about truth?"

However, Jesus' statement, "Everyone who is of truth hears My voice," raises the philosophical issue of the law of non-contradiction. Jesus is saying that anyone who has been enlightened by truth will hear his teaching (voice). Likewise anyone who hears his teaching will live in accordance with it. If Jesus' teaching therefore is right (true), then anything conflicting with it cannot be true.

This fundamental reality emanating from Jesus became the hallmark of civilizations that came under the revolutionary influence of Christianity. This concept was embedded in Judaism, and Jesus often drew on it as he challenged the religious leaders regarding their traditions. This concept, through natural revelation, dominated philosophy from ancient Greece through the Romantic period of Western civilization. Thus, our Founding Fathers, Christians or not, were guided by this fundamental concept. The Christian Founders were largely informed by the clergy. Thus, truth for our Founding Fathers was stuffed with the content of Christianity. This truth provided clarity of thinking in the framing of the principles of our nation. These principles have enabled us to determine right and wrong in the host of issues arising over the 200-plus years of our existence.

Francis Schaeffer observed, "It was the German philosopher, Hegel, who became the first man to open the door into the line of despair [the intellectual place where man is left in confusion]." He goes on to explain, "Before this, in epistemology [the science of knowing], man always thought in terms of antithesis. . . . That is the first step in classical logic. In antithesis, if this is true, then its opposite is not true."[4]

---

[4]   Francis Schaeffer, *He is There and He is Not Silent,* 20, 45.

Today we are experiencing the full impact of this Hegelian earthquake.[5] On many levels truth is no longer a stable reality. Rather *truth* and its *antithesis* modulate into a *synthesis*. The original truth is destroyed and the idea that all truth is relative has replaced it. This, for example, has given rise to social jurisprudence (law). The truth that abortion is wrong is synthesized with the "right of a woman over her own body." The synthesis being that abortion is legal (right) when performed within the parameters of the law.

As Christians, God has called us not to simply enjoy the fruits of our republic. We must educate ourselves regarding the theological, and thereby the philosophical underpinnings of our existence. We must learn to be apologists (I Peter 3:15) who can articulate these realities. We must live lives that affirm truth. We must hold public servants to the test of the law of contradiction. Christian Patriots are best equipped to resist postmodernism and educate the general public regarding the law of antithesis.

Prayer:
Father, thy word is truth! Sanctify us by thy truth (John 17:17)! Invigorate our desire to study your Word, to live the truth, to speak the truth, and to die for the truth. At stake is your glory, the Gospel of Grace, and the gift of freedom you have entrusted to us. Grant us, Father, the passion of the apostles, the faith of the Hall of Famers (Hebrews 11), the determination of the Reformers, and the commitment of our Founding Fathers that you may once more turn "the world upside down."

---

[5]   In his book, *Escape from Reason*, Francis Schaeffer cites Rousseau, Kant, Hegel, and Kierkegaard as the major contributors to this shift in philosophical framework leading the world to despair—adrift in the sea of relativism. (40-41).

Action Steps:

ACTION STEP 1

Date Completed _____
Outcome

ACTION STEP 2

Date Completed _____
Outcome

ACTION STEP 3

Date Completed _____
Outcome

Week 9   Date: _____
Your Worldview Makes a Difference!
Text: *Haggai 2:10–23*

Weekly Reading:
The Lord instructs Haggai to ask the priests two questions concerning the law. First, if a priest carries meat dedicated to be a sacrifice in the fold of his garment and that priest touches other foods, does that make the other foods holy? The answer was "no." The second question regarded the results of touching a dead body. If someone who is unclean by contact with a dead body touches any food (v. 13), does it become unclean? The answer was "yes." Haggai then proclaims the judgment of God, "So it is with this people . . . and what they offer there is unclean."

There is a principle here that we desperately need to grasp. When we touch that which is unclean we contaminate that which we subsequently touch. In the life of America we can see this principle played out in one institution after another. Two examples from Colonial America are Harvard and Princeton. Both universities were established with a Christian worldview for the purpose of training clergy and Christian civic leaders. In less than 100 years, Harvard veered from this Christian worldview under the first non-clergyman to become president, John Leverett. He led the university toward intellectual independence from Puritanism and the Christian worldview.[6] As for Princeton, this struggle between two worldviews saw its pinnacle in the debates between the college president, James McCosh, and the head of Princeton Seminary, Charles Hodge, over the question of the Darwin theory of evolution (1860s-1870s).

This struggle and the aftermath of the departure from the Christian worldview can be traced over and over again in American culture. Two more examples and their consequences will illustrate this.

The first has been the gradual shift in our judicial system from a philosophy of law rooted in the Judeo-Christian tradition to Natural Law Theory, which has led us to sociological jurisprudence. Social law is the contaminated soil out of which came legalized abortion and no-fault divorce. The second was the shift from our understanding of the origin of Scripture. The publication of Julius Wellhausen's *The Composition of the Hexateuch* (1877) marked the intellectual march toward a secularized view of Scripture.

---

6   Neil Brody Miller, "'Proper Subjects for Public Inquiry': The First Unitarian Controversy and the Transformation of Federalist Print Culture," *Early American Literature* 2008 43(1): 101–35.

The contamination has generated a widespread cultural shift away from the Christian worldview in the halls of seminaries and the pulpits of churches.

Christian Patriots, in the tradition of our Founding Fathers, must hearken back to the Scriptures that gave them their foundation—their Christian worldview. It is this worldview that fomented liberty. Touch the unclean (a secular worldview) and we contaminate the Christian worldview and thereby diminish its power to sustain liberty. The apostle Paul offered us this warning in Colossians: "Beware lest any man spoil [make you unclean] through philosophy [a non-Christian explanation of our existence and purpose] and vain deceit [taking pride in putting our understanding of the world and life above Revelation]." Just prior to this warning, Paul assures us, "In whom [Christ] are hidden all the treasures of wisdom and knowledge . . . ." Whether in hard science or social science, it is the Christian worldview that brings liberty and justice. Seek therefore to exercise your liberty to vote through the grid of a Christian Patriot's worldview.

Prayer:
O, Lord, you said, "I am the way, the truth, and the life." Today we would thank you for showing us the way to the Father, the truth by which we can interpret our world and the life that is eternal. Lord, thank you that you have given us everything we need for life and godliness. Help us to be faithful to proclaim the truth, to be prepared to give a reason for the hope within and to live everyday life out of the context of the prospect of eternal life. Amen.

Action Steps:

ACTION STEP 1 **Date Completed** _____ **Outcome**   **ACTION STEP 2**   **Date Completed** _____ **Outcome**   **ACTION STEP 3**   **Date Completed** _____ **Outcome**

Week 10
Date: _____
Woe to the Oppressors
Text: *Micah 2:1–13*

Weekly Reading:
As I write today, in the spring of 2011, Syria is the latest of a series of Arab countries to be on the verge of collapse. There are numerous reasons for this cultural upheaval (as it has come to be known, Arab Spring), but one that is common to all of them is that these nations have been suppressed by a few rich and dictatorial families who have prospered at the expense of the masses. The masses have finally tired of the injustice and have risen in protest.

Micah could be a contemporary reporter. The rich of his day were working by dishonest means to increase their wealth. To be sure, the Bible is not against wealth. Abraham, Isaac, and Jacob were wealthy. Wealthy peers supported Jesus and the disciples. In itself there is nothing wrong with prosperity. It is, in fact, a blessing to those who have wealth and to the many they bless with their wealth. Ask the likes of James McDonald, Jerry Falwell, or Billy Graham about the extent to which they and their ministries were blessed by wealth.

However, increasing one's wealth at the expense of the population through force, fraud, and other illegitimate means is not only evil but contains within it the seeds of destruction. This has been so evident in the most recent developments in the Near East. The picture that Micah paints is that of the wealthy lying awake in bed dreaming up schemes and then rushing out at the break of day to implement them. He then observes that they had forgotten that God had plans as well and that his plans would prevail. While the rich plan iniquity, God is planning disaster against them and they will not escape. History has demonstrated again and again that men like Hosni Mubarak (former president of Egypt), who have gathered wealth on the backs of the poor, earn their consequences.

In the Jerusalem of Micah's day, the wicked were defrauding a man of his home and fellow men of their inheritance (v. 2). Their energies were dedicated to developing schemes to achieve their ends. When we read this account, and that of Amos 8:4–6, we cannot but see the similarities to the Wall Street debacle of recent years, culminating in the housing and mortgage crash.

So what does this have to do with Christian Patriots? Micah was warning the southern kingdom of Judah that, since they were doing the same things for which God had punished the northern kingdom, they should not think they would be exempt from similar punishment. Micah uses the word *covets* to describe their activity. In doing so, he calls them back to Exodus 20:17, in which God commands them not to covet another man's wife, house, or servants.

As Christian Patriots, we need to expose such schemes. We must work for legislation that protects the innocent. We must cry out against the government when it devises laws that foster unfair taxation or improper use of eminent domain. We must follow the example of Micah. In doing so, we join God in seeking justice and we ensure our existence as a democratic republic because, at a national level, we follow the second greatest commandment to love our neighbor as we love ourselves.

Prayer:
Almighty God, giver of the Ten Commandments, enable us by your Holy Spirit to be keepers of the law. Help us to have the courage to proclaim your law. Convict us of our responsibility to protect all men but especially the poor. Grant us the ability to be merciful, kind and gentle. But, also, give us the strength to punish the wicked when they break the law. Help us to value the freedom you have granted us. Amen!

Action Steps:

ACTION STEP 1

Date Completed _____
Outcome

ACTION STEP 2

Date Completed _____
Outcome

ACTION STEP 3

Date Completed _____
Outcome

Week 11   Date: _____
The Value of our Heritage
Text: *Job 40:1–42:6*

Weekly Reading:
I am writing this entry three days after the massive tornado *attack* in Alabama in the spring of 2011. If you did not personally tour these areas, you cannot imagine the destruction. The pictures displayed on television and the news could not do justice to the reality. The governor of Alabama is from Tuscaloosa. You could hear the grief in his voice as he did a news conference from McFarland Avenue, where an entire Hobby Lobby shopping mall was destroyed. The beautiful restored historical district of the city of Cullman was left in shambles in a matter of minutes.

That night, I thought about how the Allies sent thousands of planes to drop tons of bombs on Germany over the duration of the war to wreak havoc. But in less than a day, the Alabama storm cut a swath up to a mile wide, for more than 180 miles. According to the Alabama Emergency Management Agency, 6,500 homes were damaged or destroyed statewide. More than 2.7 million cubic yards of debris was generated. It has been interesting and disappointing to listen to some evangelical preachers attempt to explain God's place in these events as a "non-role." One local pastor of a large evangelical church commented something like this, "Well, you know God set up the forces of nature and now he lets it run." I wonder whether he realized that he was espousing a Deist concept of our world.

But our purpose in this devotional is not about giving a proper theology of the forces of nature. It is about the value of our heritage as a nation. Much of what we consider today is true of a variety of Western nations that have been impacted by the Judeo-Christian ethic. However, the focus here is America. How is it that, within hours, citizens of Alabama were fanning out across stricken areas seeking to assist those directly impacted by the storm? A young man I know well received a call that a friend's home had been destroyed. He made his way some 40–50 miles to where neighbors were attempting to rescue this family. They found the father dead. His children's report of the father's heroism would have earned him a Medal of Honor if he had been a soldier in battle. The young man worked with this family to see that they were housed, and then shepherded the widow through the mounds of legal details over the next several days.

However, this story, in one telling or another, can be repeated hundreds of times all along the course of the storm. In fact, just a week or so earlier, a lesser set of storms rushed across the state and generated similar stories. Our church hosted several hundred women who prepared more than 3000 lunches to be distributed to needy survivors as well as rescue workers. There are plans to repeat this effort weekly as needed. Just weeks before all this occurred, the American government, as well as mission agencies and many corporations, funneled incredible volumes of aid into Japan to assist with the aftermath of its earthquake and tsunami.

From whence does this American spirit of mercy, care, and generosity arise? It emanates from the theological foundations on which America stands. It is not a matter of the spirit of man. It is not a matter of being good. It is driven by the same theological heritage that gave birth to the Constitution and the Bill of Rights. Yes, there is an American spirit, but that spirit is derived from God. It is from God that we learned to care about our neighbor. Remember what Jesus said, "Love your neighbor as you love yourself." None of us lacks self-love. Jesus reached right to the very heart of our selfishness to give us a standard for how we are to love our neighbor. Because of the incredible influence of the Gospel at the heart of America, as a culture we have internalized the concept of loving our neighbor. I for one am grateful that these tragic events become occasions to remind us of our God-given heritage of communal mercy, as well as the opportunity to practice and extend it.

Prayer:
Almighty God, the magnitude of the power of this storm reminds us that your Almighty power far exceeds what we have beheld and are yet to behold. You created this world with a spoken word. Yet, Lord, the greatest exercise of your power was loosed at Calvary when Jesus said, "It is finished!" Father, this same Jesus commanded us to love our neighbor as we love ourselves. Help us to practice this command both in our human relationships and in our civil responsibilities. Amen.

Action Steps:

ACTION STEP 1

Date Completed _____
Outcome

ACTION STEP 2

Date Completed _____
Outcome

ACTION STEP 3

Date Completed _____
Outcome

Week 12   Date: _____
Training the Next Generation
Text: *Deuteronomy 6:1–14*

Weekly Reading:
My wife has often observed that, just in our lifetime, there has been a significant diminishing of common sense. For example, when I was a boy my mother taught me that "birds of a feather flock together." She would quote this when she was attempting to teach me how to pick my friends. The quotation did not need much amplification. People understood this common sense pithy saying. Unfortunately, I was rapidly becoming a part of the population that was diminishing in common sense, and for years I ignored the lesson she was teaching me.

Where did all this common sense originate in America? It was the result of the basic teachings of the Bible being appropriately taught to succeeding generations. In our passage today, we see Moses laying out for the Israelites a basic plan of training for the youth of the coming generation. Our forefathers understood this passage in Deuteronomy. They practiced what Moses laid out for Israel. We would do well to recapture this model of training the next generation, both regarding the Christian walk and concerning American political realities. Here are the steps laid out by Moses:

1. Lay a THEOLOGICAL FOUNDATION (v. 4). This is what we find in verse four. "Hear, O Israel! The Lord is our God, the Lord is one!" Teach your children the character of God.

2. Build A RELATIONSHIP with God (v. 5). "And you shall love the Lord your God . . . ."

3. Practice BIBLICAL MEDITATION (v.6). The word "meditation" means "to talk oneself through." The idea is to take a passage of God's Word and talk out loud through its meaning and application.

4. Conduct FORMAL INSTRUCTION (v. 7a). "You shall teach them diligently." Using various methods such as a catechism (a summary of doctrine), formally instruct your children.

5. Practice CASUAL APPLICATION (7b). "You shall talk of them . . . ." As you progress through life, look for opportunities precipitated by life experiences to casually teach children through the application of biblical principles to real situations.

6. Practice INTENTIONAL APPRECIATION for God and his Word (v. 7c). "When you walk by the way . . . ." As you walk along, experiencing the realities of life, be intentional to point out where God intersects with the contingencies of life.

7. Utilize GOD'S WORD and do GOD'S WORK as a bookend to your days (v. 7d). "When you lie down and when you rise up . . . ." Open the day with a discussion of God's involvement in life and close the day with reminiscing about the evidence of God in the events of the day.

8. Display the reality of God through ARTISTIC EXPRESSION (v. 9). "Bind them . . . on your hand . . . write them on the doorposts . . . ." Artistic expression of truth is an aid to learning.

9. Guard YOUR HEART so that you do not lose a passion for this reality (vv. 10–14). "Watch yourself, lest you forget the Lord who brought you from the land of Egypt . . . ." It is imperative to keep a close watch on ourselves, lest we forget.

The manner of training our young people regarding the gifts that God has given to us in the form of our Constitution and Bill of Rights is the same model that Moses gave Israel (and the church) to preserve the knowledge of God. As Christian Patriots, we must catechize our youth both in the Scriptures and in the founding documents of our nation.

Prayer:
Holy Father, giver of all good gifts, help us to be faithful to train the next generation to appreciate the great gifts that you have given to us. Enable us to give to our children and our children's children the knowledge and wisdom that you have given to us from your Word. Amen.

Action Steps:

ACTION STEP 1

Date Completed _____
Outcome

ACTION STEP 2

Date Completed _____
Outcome

ACTION STEP 3

Date Completed _____
Outcome

Week 13   Date: _____
The Flag and the Sanctuary
Text: *Numbers 21:1-18*

Weekly Reading:
Many churches have American flags displayed on their platforms. Have you ever asked yourself why? For a number of Christians, this practice is a problem. Their view is that we need to keep the church and the state separate. As we do not allow prayer in the schools, so we should not allow the flag in the church. Our thoughts today are not about flag advocacy. They are about the relationship of the church and the state.

It is not possible for the Christian to separate church and state. Why? It is because Jesus and Paul taught us that we are responsible to live as Christians everywhere. "Whatsoever your hand finds to do, do it heartily as unto the Lord" (Col. 3:23). The question is, if I am a senator or state legislator, am I to be Christian in that arena? The answer is "yes." We have had American presidents who did this well and we have had presidents who have done this poorly. If you are the CEO of a large company and you are a believer, you are a Christian who is the CEO. So it is with a president, a senator, or any other public official.

Ok, you say, I can see that line of reasoning, but what about American flags in the sanctuary? Flags are symbols. Remember the brazen serpent? Israel complained to the point that God sent fiery serpents among them. As the people cried in repentance, God told Moses to put a brazen serpent on a pole. As people looked upon it they were healed. Jesus cites this as a symbol. As the serpent was lifted up, so must the Son of Man be lifted up (John 3:14), and as those in the wilderness exercised faith and looked upon the brazen serpent and were healed, so will those who look upon the Son of Man by faith be healed of the Serpent's *bite*. The Bible uses many symbols to teach truth. So we should use symbols to teach truth.

The American flag is the symbol of God's blessing on this nation. It reminds us that God gave us this country at the cost of much shed blood. It reminds us of how our forefathers struggled and sought God's intervention as they hammered out the Constitution and the Bill of Rights. It reminds us that the preaching of the Word of God touched innumerable lives with the Gospel and the Christian worldview. The Christian flag is also a symbol. It, too, is a manmade symbol, but nonetheless a spiritual symbol. It reminds us that we are Christians first. It reminds us that our relationship to Christ demands both our loyal submission and our obligation to impact our world with the message of the Gospel. It reminds us to worship. And it reminds us that every good and perfect gift comes from God—including our national existence and our freedom.

So, the next time someone questions you (or you question), "Why do we have the American flag on the church platform?" you will have an answer. It resides there as a symbol of the horizontal blessing of God, just as the Christian flag resides there as a symbol of the vertical blessing of God. We live in the Kingdom of God through the shed blood of the Lord Jesus. We live in America through the shed blood, sacrifice, and commitment of our forefathers through whom God gave us the gift of political and religious freedom.

Prayer:
Gracious God, giver of every good and perfect gift, we humbly thank you for Jesus and His commitment to endure the cross for the joy that was set before Him, the redemption of His church. And we thank you for our forefathers who endured the turmoil and trauma of the birthing of this nation. Grant us, Father, the endurance necessary to serve you well both as a citizen of your kingdom and a citizen of this nation.

Action Steps:

ACTION STEP 1

Date Completed _____
Outcome

ACTION STEP 2

Date Completed _____
Outcome

ACTION STEP 3

Date Completed _____
Outcome

Week 14   Date: _____
The Desire for Peace
Text: *John 14*

Weekly Reading:
The desire for peace is common among Christian Patriots. We desire peace between nations. We desire peace between our citizens. We desire peace within the church. Yet we find peace ever elusive at every level. Our passage today suggests that if we define peace correctly, we have access to peace in the midst of turmoil. In this passage Jesus promises that we can access peace through four avenues which emanate from him.

1. *The Peace of Hope* (vv. 1–3): As Christian Patriots, we often find our peace disquieted because of the threats to the standard of living to which we have become accustomed. In these verses Jesus is pointing the way to peace by refocusing us on the eternal. The temporal standard of living will be degraded (the mortgage debacle); its demise is inevitable (2 Peter 3:10). However, Jesus gives us the hope that he is building an eternal building for us in his Father's house where we will dwell in his presence. He roots this hope in his oneness with the Father (vv. 10–11).

2. *The Peace of Faith* (vv. 10–15): Faith begins with a belief in the Trinity. "Do you not believe that I am in the Father, and the Father is in me?" Jesus asks. I paraphrase: "You have lived and walked with me as well as listened to me for three years. Have you not realized that I am more than a human being? Have you not come to the realization that I am God? If not from my teaching, then surely my works have witnessed that the Father abiding in me does His works!" (vv. 10–11). Christian Patriots find peace through faith in Jesus Christ, not through our Founding Fathers and the documents upon which our temporal way of life stands. We find peace by faith in Jesus, and we encourage our faith through our works (v. 12), our prayer (vv. 13–14), and our obedience (v. 14).

3. *The Peace of Promise* (vv. 16–26): Appreciation for the promise of the Holy Spirit is essential for the Christian Patriot, lest the calamitous political turmoil overcome ur. Jesus refers to this promise as "another Helper . . . the Spirit of truth . . . [who] abides with

you" (v. 16–17). The work of this Helper, the Holy Spirit, is to be our teacher, and He will prompt our memories of all that Jesus taught (vv. 26).

4. *The Peace of Knowledge* (vv. 27–31): Jesus exhorts the disciples, and therefore us, not to let our hearts be troubled. When banks are failing, wars are raging, political entities are collapsing, and earthquakes are erupting, Jesus reminds us that he has given us the knowledge ["And now I have told you before it comes to pass, that when it comes to pass, you may believe"] to rest in the peace he has given to us (vv. 27).

The Christian Patriot must first of all be a Christian. Without the knowledge that flows from the Word of God, a Patriot will live in constant frustration and fear. Without the promised Holy Spirit living within to be the Helper, the Patriot will not have the capacity to process the frustrations of a faltering America. Without the faith to believe that Jesus is the Son of God, the Patriot will not have the framework to support the foundational documents of our republic. Without the foregoing, he will not have hope in the midst of a disintegrating nation. But With these, he will have the strength to engage the political realities with confidence.

Prayer:
Father, thank you for the peace that has come through the Prince of Peace. Thank you for your Holy Spirit who dwells within to lead me into all truth. Thank you for the knowledge of your Word to teach me discernment, direction, and determination as a Christian Patriot. Grant me, Father, the faith to take you at your word that I might experience the peace you have promised in the midst of the inevitable tumultuous times.

Action Steps:

ACTION STEP 1

Date Completed _____
Outcome

ACTION STEP 2

Date Completed _____
Outcome

ACTION STEP 3

Date Completed _____
Outcome

Week 15   Date: _____
Raise My Taxes!
Text: *I Samuel 8:10–17*

Weekly Reading:
When is the last time you heard a citizen crying out in the public square, "Raise my taxes!"? This is precisely what happened in Illinois in the spring of 2010. What possibly could motivate such incredulous behavior? That is similar to the question the average reader has when perusing the account of the Israelites besieging Samuel for a king, to be like the nations around them. Why would they want a man to be their king when they already had the God of the universe as their king? The answer is that the people were unhappy with their freedom and the accompanying responsibility under a theocracy. They wanted a king, like the nations around them, to tell them what to do. God warns them through Samuel that they will come under the dominance of the king in our passage toda). The people respond, "No, but there shall be a king over us . . . to fight our battles."

Look at who these people were in Illinois. They were public employees. They were members of a union, [a sometimes-necessary component of society that aims to bring a balance between the interest of industry and the interest of workers] What has evolved in the public sector is an organization of public employees, whose wages and benefits outstrip the private sector, for the sake of collective bargaining to maintain their economic status at any cost. So what motivated them to board buses and descend on the capital of Illinois with the war cry, "Raise my taxes!" The answer is found by traveling to New Jersey where the governor, in an effort to take control of a budget spiraling downward in debt, was curtailing spending that would result in the loss of jobs in the arena of public service union territory. So the war cry "Raise my taxes!" is the preemptive strike of union leadership who convinced their members that it is better to raise taxes to temporarily sustain a failed system than to cut social service budgets to correct the failing system and preserve a state.

My mother, my civics teacher in high school, and my college professor of the History of Civilization all sounded the same alarm. Study history and learn from the mistakes of others, or you will repeat history. It seems to me that the history of Israel teaches that if we exchange freedom under God with its accompanying personal responsibility for the assurance of government to provide cradle-to-grave care, we sacrifice freedom to gain servitude.

In the Illinois case, what is most disturbing is the fact that this narrow segment of society is not saying, "Raise my taxes for my benefit." But, they are saying, "Raise everybody's taxes for my benefit." In effect, they are petitioning the government to institute taxation without representation. Why does anyone wonder why the Tea Party movement gained momentum?

In our democratic republic, the Constitution and the Bill of Rights are to us what the God-given law was to Israel in a theocratic kingdom. To dismantle these historical documents either by neglect or by activist courts is to replace them with a "king" that will rule for the benefit of power. Our very existence as America is dependent on two things. The first is the proclamation of the Gospel, which seeds our population with God-fearing citizens. The second is the guarding and enforcement of the Constitution and Bill of Rights as they were given in their historical context.

Prayer:
O, God of heaven and earth, sometimes our American individualism blinds us from seeing our social responsibility to ensure justice. We would ask that you open our eyes to see where we have failed to care for and assist those less blessed than we. But, Lord, deliver our nation from the foolishness of becoming a "nanny state." Enable us to guard, protect, and submit to the good gifts of these historical documents. Amen.

Action Steps:

ACTION STEP 1

Date Completed _____
Outcome

ACTION STEP 2

Date Completed _____
Outcome

ACTION STEP 3

Date Completed _____
Outcome

Week 16   Date: _____
Shoeless Soldiers
Text: *Deuteronomy 29:1–9*

Weekly Reading:
From my reading of history, George Washington waged war for American freedom under the same constraints as modern military leaders: namely, wrongheaded policies of congress. Politicians attempting to manage the details of running the war without the knowledge of either the realities of the situation or the skills to manage the enterprise plagued the general. Furthermore, a sufficient number of the congress held to the mistaken belief that merchants should not make money on the war effort. One writer commented something like this: the emotion of patriotism alone should be the motivating factor, from politicians, to businessmen, to army privates.

A survey of history reveals an astounding situation. It is said that one general wrote to Washington saying his men were more fit for a hospital bed than an army camp. Others informed Washington that their men lacked heavy coats, and some even shirts. As one reads these accounts he can only conclude that these men who won our freedom were destitute of all creature comforts appropriate to their time.[7]

The stories of the shoeless soldiers with inadequate clothing and blankets generated carping and griping by these same congressmen who would not allow a free market to produce the supplies. In turn, General Washington was blamed for the desertions and poor performance on the battlefields.

While there are no direct parallels between "Your clothes have not worn out on you, and your sandals have not worn off your feet" (Deut 29:5) and the condition of Washington's men, there are parallels between the carping of the leadership and the complaining of the people toward Moses (Exodus 15–16, 32; Numbers 16). Moses, under God's immediate direction, was leading the people out of bondage—slavery is the ultimate form of taxation. Washington, under God's mediated direction, was leading our nation out of bondage from a ruler and a system teetering on the brink of a type of slavery. God did not miraculously sustain the clothing and shoes of the Continental Army, but He did sustain the Army. As God vindicated Moses and his leadership, so God affirmed the leadership of Washington. In spite of

---

[7]   The historical realities cited here are not direct citations but gleanings from readings of the internet, books, and documentaries.

a congress that lacked leadership on many fronts, God used these men and numerous others to forge a system of government based on a Constitution and Bill of Rights that guarantee each citizen freedom and the pursuit of happiness.

If we desire our children and our grandchildren to enjoy the gift of this Constitution, we must engage with this Continental Army. The war was won to secure this document and the freedoms it secured. But we are faced with increasingly strong guerrilla operations that would trash it. We must take our responsibility for leadership and engage in the process of self-governing. As Christian Patriots, we hold the mantle of this army; we are not Democrats or Republicans, Independents or Tea Partiers—we are the Shoeless Soldiers, the Continental Army of Christian Patriots, upholding God and the Constitution of our country.

Prayer:
Father in heaven, our forefathers prayed that your will be done on earth as it is in heaven. Then they set out to do your will on earth. They preached, they prayed, they engaged themselves in the task of addressing all of life through a biblical worldview. As you were pleased to use them to give us a free America and the freedom to preach the Gospel and worship you, so use us to participate and sustain this nation that your will may be done for generations from this staging field called America. Amen.

Action Steps:

ACTION STEP 1

Date Completed _____
Outcome

ACTION STEP 2

Date Completed _____
Outcome

ACTION STEP 3

Date Completed _____
Outcome

Week 17   Date: _____
Stopping Tyranny is Costly
Text: *Matthew 27; Revelation 19–20*

Weekly Reading:
Stopping the machine of tyranny is costly. In his wonderful book, *War Letters: Extraordinary Correspondence from American Wars*, Andy Carroll gives us a glimpse of this cost through the eyes of soldiers. Here are two examples from World War II:

Carroll captures the observations of a captain who was the Chief of Surgery at the Pearl Harbor Naval Hospital on December 7, 1941. He describes the gruesome sight of hundreds of casualties pouring into the hospital. "It was hell for a while," he remembers.

The picture he paints is the picture of modern warfare. Men suffering gunshot wounds administered morphine while thrashing in pain. Some triaged and left to die while others were patched up heal to fight again.

"Without faith, I don't see how anyone could stand this," commented a soldier named Paul Curtis. Every negative emotion—anger, disgust, loneliness, hunger, thirst, hate, and homesickness all wound up together—describes the experience of a man at war.[8]

Civil War General William Tecumseh Sherman, from the Union Army, is credited with the saying, "War is Hell!" Satan has focused the fury of hell on the world since the fall of Adam and Eve. The carnage of war is strewn across the face of history. The ravages of sexual abuse and the suppression of women are evident in every society on earth. Murder, treachery, sexual deviation, and every kind of deception have punctuated human relationships throughout recorded history.

While America has fallen prey to all these evils at one time or another, her Christian underpinnings forged a nation in which the rule of law pushed back the forces of evil with more vigor than ever before. The Ten Commandments became the symbol of our existence. They are quoted or referenced in some form or another on public buildings throughout the nation. While they do not secure full obedience or anything near public righteousness, they are a constant reminder of our goals to form a more perfect union and to provide an environment in which every person can pursue happiness.

---

8   Andy Carroll, *War Letters: Extraordinary Correspondence from American Wars* (New York: Scribner, 2002).

The fury of hell has been blunted by two forces in America: the public display of the Ten Commandments and the redemptive work of Christ proclaimed in every settlement, village, city, and state. America has been committed to stopping tyranny. She has paid the high price of her sons on battlefields and policemen on her streets. Many others have spent their lives and fortunes in the defense of righteousness in myriad ways.

Christian Patriots cannot relinquish the fight to push back evil. We must serve our beloved country at the polls, in politics, in the business world, in the military, and in every other walk of life. But we must always remember that this service is a sub-set of our service in the Kingdom of Christ. "That the gates of hell will not prevail" is the promise of Jesus Christ himself, because He paid the ultimate price to stop the tyranny. We must press forward with the Gospel, out of which flows ultimate freedom and righteousness.

Prayer:
O Lord, it is with grateful hearts that we call ourselves Americans. It is from hearts full of praise that we call ourselves Christians. We thank you that at the cross the fury of hell for us was poured out on Jesus. We thank you that the gates of hell will not prevail because Jesus has already won the victory. We thank you that we now serve you when we serve our country, even as we live and proclaim the Gospel to a lost world. Amen!

Action Steps:

ACTION STEP 1

Date Completed _____
Outcome

ACTION STEP 2

Date Completed _____
Outcome

ACTION STEP 3

Date Completed _____
Outcome

Week 18   Date: _____
My Vote Can Still Count!
Text: *2 Timothy 3:1–4*

Weekly Passage:
How does a Christian Patriot evaluate a candidate? I am a patriot, not a politician. I am not a fan of intentional political careers. The candidate who appeals to me is the individual who has these five earmarks:

1. Personal character evidenced by integrity in business and fidelity in relationships
2. Documentary integrity evidenced by a historical and grammatical interpretation of the Constitution and our other founding documents
3. Financial conservatism evidenced by a commitment to a balanced budget and minimal taxation
4. Decentralized government from the federal level downward
5. Encouragement in and facilitation of compassionate care for those in need

Unfortunately, when pursuing the landscape of candidates, more times than not the following characteristics surface:

1. Lovers of self—what is good for me is predominant
2. Covetous—a desire to have the power and prestige of others
3. Boasters—look at what I did for the district
4. Proud—I am a greater leader, and you should do what I tell you is good for you
5. Disobedient—like children to parents, candidates frequently bend the rules of society
6. Unthankful—preoccupation with personal agenda demonstrates unthankfulness toward constituencies
7. Unholy—from sexual immorality to bribery and lying, unholy behavior bubbles to the top repeatedly
8. Traitors—pushing one-world government at the sacrifice of American sovereignty
9. High-minded—thinking more highly of themselves and their ideas than they ought
10. Lovers of pleasure—a common trait of our society

If you are a reader of the Bible you recognize this list of characteristics. They appear in Paul's description of the latter days (2 Tim. 3:2, 4). I am not entering into a discussion of eschatology; I am simply pointing out that what we are dealing with is not contemporary; rather, it is the perpetual condition of mankind. It is our generation's responsibility to endure, to fight the good fight of faith. It is our generation's responsibility to sift and sort the best candidates from the rubble of humanity. We live in a society where God has given us the responsibility to participate in our governing. To exercise this responsibility we must define our values and our *earmarks*, and discern those candidates who correlate while displaying the least serious defects of a fallen humanity.

The biggest challenge in rising to this responsibility is the disinformation that pervades the process. A liberal administration gives rise to a bumper crop of conservatives. However, for many candidates this is simply a public relations move to distance them from the sitting liberal president. This generates confusion for those who are attempting to sift and sort among the candidates to make an informed decision. Each of us who genuinely care and accept responsibility for the governing process must relentlessly evaluate the candidates. Unfortunately, we can expect little help from the mainstream media.

Prayer:
Lord, grant us wisdom to discern between character and public relations rhetoric. Grant us the determination to pursue truth. Grant that your Spirit would open the minds and hearts of those in power to examine their motives and determine their character. Finally, Lord, grant us repentance wherein we have failed in our responsibility for self-governing through engaging in the system that you have gracious gifted to us.

Action Steps:

ACTION STEP 1

Date Completed _____
Outcome

ACTION STEP 2

Date Completed _____
Outcome

ACTION STEP 3

Date Completed _____
Outcome

Week 19   Date: _____
National Humility
Text: *Deuteronomy 29*

Weekly Passage:
America as a nation, and citizens as individuals, desperately need to implement humility (I Peter 5:6). America has become arrogant. We have taken it more and more on ourselves to determine right and wrong. We have incorporated the flaw of Israel during the period of the Judges, "Every man did that which was right in his own eyes," into a legal system. Thus, abortion is legal. No-fault divorce encourages the quick dissolution of marriages. The federal government has sanctioned avaricious business practices that push our economy to the brink of destruction. Legalized gambling is a creeping crud that threatens to become a national pastime. Credible reports say, for example, that $10 billion was wagered on the 2011 Super Bowl alone. Most of this was done illegally, but it faced little law enforcement intervention.

God's covenant with Israel was contained in the book of the law of God (Deut. 29:20). There was a theocratic relationship between God and Israel that is not true of God and America. However, there are theological principles that form the foundation of this book of the law of God, and these are applicable to America (or any nation that would establish its existence on the Word of God). These theological principles, while not specific promises, have a functional reality. This reality is that the nation that will formulate its laws and social relationships consistent with these principles will reap the blessing of God.

Most of our forefathers understood this reality and formulated our Constitution and Bill of Rights to reflect these principles. This is why it is so important that our Constitution is interpreted historically, grammatically, and philosophically within the context of its development. Only in this manner will we preserve the theological principles that lead to God's blessings.

So what does all this mean for us today? I, writing this, and you, reading this, are only two people among hundreds of millions. Even if we were two United States senators, we would only be two people with little more influence. So, I repeat, what does all of this mean for us today? Let me suggest several things.

First, it means that we must choose to live according to what is right in God's eyes. Second, it means that we will commit ourselves to pray for repentance like Daniel of old. Third, it means we must seek out and vote for those at every level of government who would seek to bring about public repentance (or at least reform). Fourth, it means that we will speak out both in church and in the public forum calling for that repentance. Fifth, where God gives the ability and the opportunity we will enter the public square to serve in academia and government offices with a commitment not to use our offices to preach, but to call our fellow Americans back to our roots. We should, however, do this in such a way that our lives preach the Gospel.

Prayer:
Father, thank you for giving to us forefathers who understood that freedom comes from God and blessings flow from righteous living that honors God and refuses to practice idolatry. Grant us the strength and courage, like Joshua of old, to walk consistently and the wisdom to avoid practicing the foolishness of worshiping on the high places while naming God as our Lord (2 Kings 17:32). Grant us to engage in repentance and honor you by serving our country in leading it to righteousness.

Action Steps:

ACTION STEP 1

Date Completed _____
Outcome

ACTION STEP 2

Date Completed _____
Outcome

ACTION STEP 3

Date Completed _____
Outcome

Week 20   Date: _____
Political Correctness Gone Awry
Text: *Isaiah 5:18–23*

Weekly Reading:
Isaiah warns, "Woe unto them that call evil good, and good evil; that put darkness for light, and light for darkness; that put bitter for sweet, and sweet for bitter!" These words of Isaiah put what we sometimes, as Christian Patriots, wave off as a silly culturalism that will soon fade. So what is political correctness, then, from a biblical perspective?

For a number of years now, political correctness has been a growing and confusing phenomenon in our society. The concept of inappropriate words and actions has long since been a part of our sociological fabric. And rightly so! What has changed in our lifetime that has resulted in calling evil good and good evil? The answer is this: we have replaced our Judeo-Christian value system with a postmodern system. This has led to both confusion and conflict, and the slow eroding of the Bill of Rights and the Constitution.

There are two arenas in which I have observed this confusion and conflict. The first is in the face of many of our political leaders. Over the last year I kept asking myself, "Why does he/she seem to be angry all the time?" The situation does not matter. Even if they are smiling or laughing, the anger seeps through. I've come to the conclusion that for them much of what is historically good about America is evil and must be eradicated while much of what is evil in American tradition must be seen as good. During the last major campaign season, speeches promised change, but change was never defined. It appears that they envisioned inverting American values. Part of the apparent anger would be their frustration with the slow progress in achieving this goal of change.

The second arena is religious freedom. Religious freedom is being morphed into religious tolerance. Religious freedom is the guarantee of our historical documents and extends to every individual the right to worship in accord with his conscience. Religious tolerance is the government giving permission for the exercise of religion. Tolerance leads to totalitarianism. This is demonstrated in a recent court decision upholding the right of Eastern Michigan University to dismiss a graduate counseling student who asked to be excused from counseling a homosexual because it violated her religious beliefs. She was told that to continue in the program it would be necessary to undergo an educational remediation plan that "would help her deal with the behavior, to learn how to deal with conflicting values and providing appropriate clinical services to people whose values she may not agree with."[9] In other words, she would have to learn how to call evil good and good evil and thereby violate her religious values, not to mention her freedom! The American Counseling Association's code of ethics was cited by the judge as the document of authority in this case. Hence, this document usurped the Bill of Rights.

So how are we to speak in this atmosphere of political correctness gone awry? Two biblical words come to mind, along with two models. First, we consider the models. Jesus gave us the model of calling a spade a spade. For example, in an exchange with the Jewish leadership he said, "You are of your father, the Devil" (certainly not politically correct). The apostles Peter and John gave us the model of priorities. They said to the authorities, "Whether it is right in the sight of God to listen to you rather than to God, you must judge, for we cannot but speak what we have seen and heard." Second, the two words that occur in the context of how a Christian should relate to others (Eph. 4:22–32) are *kind* and *tenderhearted*. Kind means gracious. It has the idea of useful or excellent. Tenderhearted means to be concerned for the feelings of the other person. The Bible sums it up as, "Speak the truth in love."

Prayer:
Father, grant us the character to call a spade a spade, but to do so with love. Grant us the determination to fight for the historical interpretation of the documents of self-government and personal rights that you gifted to us through our Founding Fathers. Grant us the faith of our fathers, like the Lollard followers of John Wycliffe, who went to the fiery trial of burning at the stake for their commitment to the Word of God. Amen!

---

9   Kyle Martin, "Judge Tosses Suit Similar to ASU Case: Homosexuality, Personal Beliefs Arise in Michigan Student Case," *The Augusta Chronicle*, Sunday July 31, 2011. http://chronicle.augusta.com/news/education/2010-08-10/asu-denies-claims-made-student. See also: http://www.emich.edu/aca_case/keypoints.php; http://speakupmovement.org/Map/CaseDetails?Case=201. A similar situation in England may be referenced at http://archbishop-cranmer.blogspot.com/2009/12/christian-teacher-sacked-as-she-is-told.html.

Action Steps:

ACTION STEP 1

Date Completed _____
Outcome

ACTION STEP 2

Date Completed _____
Outcome

ACTION STEP 3

Date Completed _____
Outcome

Week 21   Date: _____
Possessing the Blessings of God
Text: *Deuteronomy 4 (particularly verses 1–6, 10, 23–24)*

Weekly Reading:
John Adams, who was of a more liberal persuasion about Christianity, wrote, "The Christian religion is . . . the religion of wisdom . . . . It is resignation to God, it is goodness itself to man." Along with a majority of the members of the Continental Congress, he viewed the Higher Law of God as the bedrock of human liberty. These men understood this principle embedded in what they viewed as the model of a covenant between God and Israel. Few, if any, viewed America as a new Israel, but they grasped the fact that woven into that covenant relationship between God and Israel was articulated a set of principles that were an expression of His character, and He would therefore honor it.

Principle 1: Listen to the statutes and commandments of God. Our forefathers understood this principle. They listened to sermons regularly. They built colleges to train preachers. They read the Bible, even using it as a school textbook to teach reading. They wove these statutes and commandments into the fabric of the foundational documents of our nation as well as our system of law.

Principle 2: Perform the statutes and commandments of God. They understood the importance of obedience. "Perform" here is synonymous with "obey." For instance, Jesus said, "If you love me you will obey me" (John 14:15).

Principle 3: Possess the land that the Lord God gives you. For our forefathers, no doubt, this had both a literal and a spiritual meaning. They were about possessing the land in the sense of developing it and unifying it into a functional nation. But for them, and for us, this also has a deeper spiritual meaning. As we listen and perform the commandments of God we can possess that joyful Christian life that God has promised to them who love Him and who are obedient to Him.

Principle 4: Transfer truth to the next generation so that they may transfer truth on to the next generation. Our forefathers understood the importance of the transference of truth. If Israel was going to survive, it had to teach the next generation what God had taught it (Deut. 4:10; cf. 4:23).

<u>Principle 5: Idolatry of any kind does not lead to freedom but bondage</u> (Deuteronomy 4:24). Whenever Israel departed from the statutes and commandments of the Lord, it turned to the bondage that eventually brought judgment and the suspension of the covenant for centuries to come. Our forefathers forged a set of documents, under Divine Providence, that provided unparalleled freedom. But if we turn to "idolatry" in some "ism," rejecting what God has given to us, and trash these founding documents, we will find ourselves in a morass of confusion, heading for destruction.

Prayer:
Almighty God who rules by Divine Providence in the affairs of men, revive us and lead us to repentance: First, for not listening to your Word and not loving you by walking in obedience to Jesus. Second, for failing to fully participate in our self-governing that you ordained for us. Third, for failing to fully and appropriately transfer the knowledge of your statutes and commandments to the next generation along with the implications of the responsibilities of self-governing with which you have graciously blessed us. Now invigorate us to remember and to revive and possess this gift and thereby capitalize on it for the evangelization of the world.

Action Steps:

ACTION STEP 1

Date Completed _____
Outcome

ACTION STEP 2

Date Completed _____
Outcome

ACTION STEP 3

Date Completed _____
Outcome

Week 22   Date: _____
The Law of God and the Constitution
Text: *Psalm 19*

Weekly Reading:
There is a great deal of controversy in the church surrounding the law of
God. For some, the law is a thing we are freed from, and we no longer have
to observe it or focus on its consequences. For others, the law is a document
to be followed fully and to the letter. For still others, the law serves the
purpose of instruction, but is not binding on the conscience. Each of these
views has some element of truth, but we often respond to the law of God
as though it were a buffet line at a restaurant, picking and choosing what
we will from it. Or, to put it another way, we respond to the law emotionally
and decide whether or not it meets our needs for the present. Interestingly,
we would not respond to the law of our land the same way. Why, therefore,
do we respond to the law of God in this fashion, particularly when God has
explained to us the use of the law?

The Scriptures teach us that the law of God has three purposes. First,
according to the apostle Paul, the law is a schoolmaster or a tutor to lead
us to Christ, so that we may be justified by faith (Gal. 3:24). The psalmist
observes that the law of the Lord is perfect and has the capacity to restore
our souls. He continues his thought, explaining that this is true because
God's testimony is certain to make us wise (Ps. 19:7). Paul and the psalmist
are playing from the same sheet music.

The second purpose of the law is to guide us in living like Christ (Ps.
119:105). How do I function as a husband or wife? How do I make ethical
decisions in a complex business environment? How do I determine for whom
to vote? How do I discern justice and measure mercy? I study God's law! In
my profession as a counselor, I often ask counselees whether they think the
Ten Commandments are negative or positive. They almost always answer
"negative." But I always respond, "No, they are positive! They are stated in
the negative, but keeping them brings a positive outcome. For example, take
the command to not commit adultery. It is positive because it protects one
from getting shot, as well as from many other complicating life issues." God's
law will enlighten our eyes (Ps. 19:8).

The third purpose of the law is to restrain sin. Again the psalmist gives
us insight when he writes that internalizing the commandments of God
restrains me from sinning against God (119:11). It was D. L. Moody who

said, "The Bible will keep me from sin, and sin will keep me from the Bible." In other words, purposefully dwelling on the law of God will have both a deterrent effect on my life and joyful effect (Ps. 19:8).

As a Christian Patriot, I therefore recognize that the law of God has three functions in our lives as citizens as well. As a subsidiary document to the Bible, the Constitution functions in a similar manner with regard to my civil life. It is a schoolmaster that drives me to civil freedom. While the Constitution does not require all citizens to have a relationship with God, when understood in the view of the Founding Fathers, it does assume that all citizens recognize that their civil freedom emanates from God. The Preamble tutors us regarding the nature and structure of our freedom.

The Constitution guides us. American history is replete with the struggles to become what we were founded to be. The Constitution and the Bill of Rights are our form and structure. But, because we are sinners, we can be no more perfect as Americans than we are as Christians. Just as there have been thousands of books written in our attempts to properly apply the Scriptures, so it is with the Constitution and Bill of Rights. Yet, we dare not abandon these foundational documents any more than we can abandon the Scriptures. We need the Scriptures to guide us in faithful Christian living. We need the Constitution and Bill of Rights to guide us in being faithful Americans.

The Constitution and Bill of Rights restrain us from falling prey to the likes of communism, socialism, and the many humanist attempts to manage our world. As meditating on the Bible restrains us from sin, so meditating on these founding documents restrains us from straying from those great aspirations expressed in the Preamble of the Constitution.

As Christians we first embrace the law of God and its threefold ministry in our lives. As Patriots we embrace the threefold utilization of these founding documents in our civil lives. In reality, it is the embracing of the law of God that enables us to be good Americans and to embrace the gift of civil freedom that God has given us.

Prayer:
O, Lord, thank you for your law that *is a lamp unto my feet* (Ps. 119:105). Thank you for your Word that guides me in Christian living. Thank you for your law that taught me my absolute need of you. Thank you that your law

was effective in the lives of our Founding Fathers to providentially form a government and society that has secured our personal freedoms, but even more importantly provided a framework for the expansion of the Kingdom of God. Grant us, O Lord, the resolve to be strong and courageous first in our commitment to your Word and then in our commitment to the integrity of our foundational documents.

Action Steps:

ACTION STEP 1

Date Completed _____
Outcome

ACTION STEP 2

Date Completed _____
Outcome

ACTION STEP 3

Date Completed _____
Outcome

Week 23   Date: _____
Leadership: Aaron and Hur
Text: *Exodus 17:8–16*

Weekly Reading:
No leader, no matter how gifted in strategy and talented in leadership, stands alone. Even leaders appointed directly by God, like Moses, or those who rise to their positions by evident Divine Providence, do not stand alone. George Washington, the father of our nation, is no exception. A comparison between Moses, with Aaron and Hur, and George Washington in this regard is enlightening.

In Exodus 17, we have a record which demonstrates that neither Moses stood alone nor did his successor. On the battlefield General Joshua fought valiantly, but when Moses grew weary and lowered his hands, Joshua lost ground to the Amalek. It was then that Aaron and Hur held up the hands of Moses, resulting in Joshua overwhelming Amalek and his people.

Friedrich Wilhelm von Steuben, also referred to as Baron von Steuben, was a Prussian-born military officer who served as a major general of the Continental Army. He is credited with turning a volunteer militia into the Continental Army by teaching them the essentials of tactics, discipline, and military drills, and in the process generating morale, confidence, and an ability to endure. He served as General Washington's chief of staff for the final years of the war. He was like an Aaron to Washington.[10]

The French general, Marquis de Lafayette, was the second man to hold up the hands of Washington. He was wounded during the Battle of Brandywine, but managed to organize a successful retreat. In the middle of the war he returned to France to negotiate an increase in French economic and military support. On his return, he blocked troops led by Cornwallis at Yorktown while the armies of Washington and Jean-Baptiste Donatien de Rochambeau prepared for battle against the British. He was like a Hur to Washington.

As we move through American history we find a number of occasions in which God, by Divine Providence, orchestrated events to affect an outcome that brought success and blessing to this nation. While America does not

---

[10]   While the contributions of von Steuben and Lafayette are rather common knowledge, a Christian perspective will be found in the book *Sacred Fire* by Peter Lillbeck.

hold the position, like Israel, as God's chosen people, she does hold the position of being divinely favored. We should never take this position for granted or see it simply for our benefit (though we have greatly benefitted), but rather recognize that God gave us the gift of our Constitution and Bill of Rights as His means of creating a Gospel-sending base of operations.

We need to pray that God will raise up another George Washington, as well as a von Steuben and Lafayette, to hold up his hands. We need to pray for God's providential intervention to bring to the presidency a statesman of moral character. We need to pray for men and women to arise in Congress who will be the Aaron and the Hur that are necessary to pass reconstructive legislation. We need to pray that the populace, in sufficient numbers, is willing to follow their leadership to infuse into our society the godly thinking that implements the Constitution and Bill of Rights in accordance with the intention of our Founding Fathers.

Prayer:
Almighty God, Governor of Providence, raise a leader of integrity who will lead the nation to repentance. Bring to the surface those who can hold up their hands so that those who are fighting the battles on the landscape of our culture can overwhelm those who would destroy the good gifts which you have given to us. Sustain our freedom so that from this nation the Light of the World might continue to shine forth and, in the process, that we might enjoy the blessing of being a free people.

Action Steps:

ACTION STEP 1

Date Completed _____
Outcome

ACTION STEP 2

Date Completed _____
Outcome

ACTION STEP 3

Date Completed _____
Outcome

Week 24   Date: _____
Let Us Pray
Text: *Romans 13*

Weekly Reading:

Many scholars contend that Ben Franklin was an Episcopalian turned Deist. Perhaps, but it may also be that he and others of the Founding Fathers were being skeptical of government entanglements with the church as they observed it in Europe, and therefore preferred a more personal religious practice. Whatever the case, the following "Let Us Pray" speech by Franklin bears witness to the fact that our Founding Fathers have intricately woven God and country into the fabric of this nation. Today, as Christian Patriots, may we be stimulated to follow their example.

> *The small progress we have made after four or five weeks close attendance & continual reasonings with each other— our different sentiments on almost every question, several of the last producing as many noes as ays, is methinks a melancholy proof of the imperfection of the Human Understanding. We indeed seem to **feel** our own wont of political wisdom, since we have been running about in search of it. We have gone back to ancient history for models of government, and examined the different forms of those Republics which having been formed with the seeds of their own dissolution now no longer exist. And we have viewed Modern States all round Europe, but find none of their Constitutions suitable to our circumstances.*

> *In this situation of this Assembly groping as it were in the dark to find political truth, and scarce able to distinguish it when to us, how has it happened, Sir, that we have not hitherto once thought of humbly applying to the Father of lights to illuminate our understandings? In the beginning of the contest with G. Britain, when we were sensible of danger we had daily prayer in this room for the Divine Protection. —Our prayers, Sir, were heard, and they were graciously answered. All of us who were engaged in the struggle must have observed frequent instances of a Superintending providence in our favor. To that kind providence we owe this happy opportunity of consulting in peace on the means of*

establishing our future national felicity. And have we now forgotten that powerful friend? or do we imagine that we no longer need His assistance.

*I have lived, Sir, a long time and the longer I live, the more convincing proofs I see of this truth—that **God** governs in the affairs of men. And if a sparrow cannot fall to the ground without his notice, is it probable that an empire can rise without his aid? We have been assured, Sir, in the sacred writings that "except the Lord build they labor in vain that build it." I firmly believe this; and I also believe that without his concurring aid we shall succeed in this political building no better than the Builders of Babel: We shall be divided by our little partial local interests; our projects will be confounded, and we ourselves shall become a reproach and a bye word down to future age. And what is worse, mankind may hereafter this unfortunate instance, despair of establishing Governments by Human Wisdom, and leave it to chance, war, and conquest.*

I therefore beg leave to move—that henceforth prayers imploring the assistance of Heaven, and its blessings on our deliberations, be held in this Assembly every morning before we proceed to business, and that one or more of the Clergy of this City be requested to officiate in that service.[11]

Prayer:

Almighty God, you who have providentially established this nation, we observe your actions on the pages of history. We thank you for granting us the privilege of this heritage. We thank you that we are free to worship you. We thank you that we are free to transmit your truth to our children. We thank you for all those whom you have raised up to birth and to protect this nation. But, most of all we thank you for the Lord Jesus Christ and his redemptive work. Our thankfulness to be Americans is far overshadowed by our thankfulness to be citizens of the Kingdom of God.

---

[11]   Copyright status: Public Domain

Action Steps:

ACTION STEP 1

Date Completed _____
Outcome

ACTION STEP 2

Date Completed _____
Outcome

ACTION STEP 3

Date Completed _____
Outcome

Week 25   Date: _____

Lord, Teach Me a Heart of Gratitude

Text: *I Corinthians 6:19–20; 7:20–24*

Weekly Reading:

"Ask not, what your country can do for you. Ask what you can do for your country." As a college student, I listened to JFK's inaugural address. At the time, this line did not ignite my imagination. More and more over the years, however, its brilliance has done so. Unfortunately his successor, Lyndon Johnson, did not grasp President Kennedy's passion. He initiated "the Great Society" and set into motion government policies that actually taught Americans to ask, "What can my country do for me?" The great wave of entitlement that plagues America with ever-increasing indebtedness has been Johnson's legacy.

Just as a person would want the best for his or her family or friends, to the point that they would try to contribute as much or more back to them as they had gained, so American citizens should desire to give back to their country. They should begin to see themselves as part of the American *family* and think of ways they can reflect all of the benefits they have enjoyed back to society just as our forefathers made sacrifices to ensure the happiness and well-being of future generations. We should, as it were, *pay it forward* to show our gratitude.

A Christian Patriot is a citizen who protects the future by honoring the tradition on which we were founded, while at the same time embracing the application of those principles to the developing contingencies of contemporary society. Our Founding Fathers could not anticipate the internet, television, and international business that occur at the speed of light. However, by God's providence they provided us a structure from which we can chart a course through the maze of our day and the days to come.

As Christian Patriots we have a parallel responsibility in God's kingdom. God has given us his Word. The sixty-six books of the Bible are a bit more than the Constitution and Bill of Rights both in their size and their importance. These books are His-story. These books are the history of redemption. Through these books runs what has been called the scarlet cord of redemption. These books tell us from whence the world came. They tell us our origin. They tell us our purpose. They tell us our destination. God has given us his Son, perfect man and perfect God, who died in our place. He paid the penalty for our sin. He rose again from the dead that we might anticipate the resurrection. God gave us everything we need for life and godliness (2 Peter 1:3). He gave us the law. He gave us his Spirit to enable us to live by his law. He instructed us how to build our character that we might become more and more like Christ.

We should not ask, "What can God do for me?" He has already done all that we need. Rather, we should be asking, "What can I do for God to express my appreciation for his great work in my life?" The Christian Patriot best serves his country when he serves God by living a godly life in every arena of life, including the exercise of civic responsibilities to participate in self-governing.

Prayer:
It is in humility, O Lord, that I pledge my allegiance to both the Christian flag and the American flag. My Lord, you have given me freedom from the slavery of sin and a new heart as a citizen of your kingdom. You have given me freedom of religion and the pursuit of happiness as an American. What else can I say than, "Lord, how can I serve you in your kingdom and how can I serve my country?"

Action Steps:

ACTION STEP 1

Date Completed _____
Outcome

ACTION STEP 2

Date Completed _____
Outcome

ACTION STEP 3

Date Completed _____
Outcome

Week 26   Date: _____
Intertwining of Spiritual and Temporal Citizenships
Text: *Acts 22:17–23:5*

Weekly Reading:
Roman citizenship at the time of the apostle Paul provided a broad umbrella of protections. Among these protections were: a right to sue, a right to a legal trial in a proper court with the ability to present a defense, a right of appeal, and even if convicted of treason a right not to die on a cross.[12] Paul was well aware of the value of his Roman citizenship and did not hesitate to appeal to it in the midst of exercising his responsibilities appertaining to his spiritual citizenship.

In the passage for our consideration today there is an interesting nuance in the Greek text not reflected in the English translation.[13] In verse 22:27, the Roman commander asked Paul whether he was a Roman, that is, a Roman citizen. In verse 28 Paul affirms that he was born a Roman citizen. The word "citizenship" in this discussion is the Greek *politeia* [πολιτεία]. In Acts 23:1 Paul says in the English translation, "I have lived my life with a perfectly good conscience before God up to this day." This English translation "have lived" misses the impact of the Greek verb that Paul uses. He picks up the theme of citizenship by using a verbal form *politeuomai* [πολιτεύομαι] of the noun used in verse 28. Hence, a more literal translation would read, "I have exercised my citizenship with a perfectly good conscience before God up to this day."[14]

With this play on words in mind it appears that the high priest was offended at the fact that Paul appeals to his Roman citizenship in a Jewish religious court. Paul's rebuke to being slapped by the Jewish court is based on his Roman citizenship and the rights guaranteed therein. When he in return is rebuked for reviling the high priest, Paul reverts to his Jewish citizenship, citing the Scripture as the basis for his rebuke.

Paul was a well-trained Pharisee who understood the intricacies of both Roman and Jewish law and how to appeal to each. Paul actually held three passports. He was a Roman citizen, a Jew, and a Christian. He did not hesitate

---

[12]   Drawn from a perusal of various sources regarding the value of Roman citizenship.
[13]   I am indebted to Dr. Andy Montgomery, Classical Professor of Stamford University, for this insight.
[14]   Logos Bible Software 4.

to play on these citizenships when it was useful to spread the Gospel. In the current situation he protects his citizenship in the Kingdom of God by exercising his Jewish citizenship and in particular his association with the Pharisees. In Acts 23:6 he cried out, "I am a Pharisee, the son of Pharisees; and I am on trial for the hope of the resurrection of the dead." Like the good lawyer that he was, he shifts the focus from the accused (himself) to the flaws in the system (religious and philosophical differences among the accusers).

Christian Patriots have both spiritual and temporal citizenships. It is neither wrong nor unwise for the Christian Patriot to utilize his temporal citizenship (or the citizenship of any nation) in his defense or the protection of his rights to preach the Gospel.

Unfortunately there are those in America who profess Kingdom of God citizenship and prostitute it for their greedy personal ends, whether money or power. But the Christian Patriot cannot react by slipping into being passive. We are under obligation to preach the Gospel. We are under obligation to worship God. We are under obligation to pray in public and private for those who rule over us. We are under obligation to be salt and light. And, if we imitate Paul as he bids us do, we are under obligation to intertwine our spiritual and temporal citizenships for the glory of God while trusting God with the outcome as he did.

Prayer:
Dear Jesus, you have taught us to be wise as serpents and harmless as doves. You have taught us that often the world is wiser than we are. Lord, guide us by your Spirit so that we may be wise and able to discern how to utilize our American citizenship to preserve our freedom to preach the Gospel. Enable us to imitate our forefathers so that we perpetuate a nation that preserves freedom for the sake of the furtherance of the Kingdom of God.

Action Steps:

ACTION STEP 1

Date Completed _____
Outcome

ACTION STEP 2

Date Completed _____
Outcome

ACTION STEP 3

Date Completed _____
Outcome

Week 27   Date: _____
Kingdom Priorities
Text: *John 21:14–25*

Weekly Reading:
We often forget that after the resurrection of Jesus, the disciples were in the dark as to what was occurring. Our position beyond that moment of history affords us certain luxuries the disciples did not have. So it is good to remember that the context of this passage is the restoration of a group of disciples who, led by Peter, had decided to quit their roles in the kingdom. Peter became frustrated with Jesus. He had left his livelihood to pursue an association with Jesus. Whether he initially perceived Jesus to be more than a rabbi with a radical message is not clear. Peter's confession during the latter half of the second year of Jesus' ministry is the first direct affirmation that Jesus is the Messiah (Matt. 16:16). There is a pattern of kingdom priorities observed in this passage. When the Christian lives by these priorities, he is also a Patriot, bringing blessing to his nation.

The prediction of his denial of Jesus (by Jesus himself), the crucifixion of the Christ, and the post-resurrection appearances of Jesus left Peter in a state of utter confusion. He became so frustrated that, in what was no doubt a hot discussion, Peter proclaims that he is finished and is returning to his trade of fishing (John 21:1–3). Others follow his leadership. The next morning Jesus appears on the shore and calls out inquiring as to the productivity of their night of fishing. He pursues them to restore them to fellowship and service.

In the process of restoration, Jesus lays out three priorities for the believer in His kingdom. This same Jesus pursues all believers when, like Peter (and the others for whom Peter is spokesman), we become frustrated and decide to go our own way. He calls us back to these priorities.

The first priority is in loving God. There are three dimensions to this main concern: priority of the love of God over family (remember some of these were brothers, and the businesses were family affairs); priority over friends (remember these men have been isolated, constant companions suffering ridicule with Jesus); and priority over trade, profession, or business.

The second priority is the call to the humility of service. Once again, Jesus uses the unflattering illustration of his people as sheep. Shepherding was one of the most humble occupations of the day. It was a smelly, lonesome, and dangerous job. Jesus calls them back into His service and uses the imperative verb tense, signifying continuing action. Shepherding is humble service that impinges constantly on the caregiver's life.

The third priority is submission to the Lordship of Christ. In this instance it is characterized as a willingness to submit to the purposes of God (v. 18–19), even when we know that doing so will cost us our lives. We are called to this submission even when we are aware that the distribution of God's gifts and assignments appear to be unfair (v. 22–24). It does not require a prophecy to know that in the contemporary American culture tending and shepherding God's sheep will bring persecution to some and not to others. Christian Patriots must support one another even as did John and Peter as they live in obedience to Christ.[15]

The Christian who implements these priorities in his relationship to the King will be an excellent Patriot. Living a committed Christian life dictates that Patriots honor and obey those who rule over them. In America the ultimate ruler is the Constitution and its Bill of Rights. We submit to these *rulers* by exercising the responsibility to participate in governing. We do this by voting and serving. Our Christian priorities guide us in executing both of these responsibilities.

Prayer:
Dear Jesus, thank you that you seek us out when we have returned to our former lives. Thank you that you demonstrate love even as you called us to love. Thank you that you demonstrate shepherding even as you call us to shepherd. Thank you for placing us in a nation in which you have secured our freedom to minister in whatever capacity you have called us. Help us, Jesus, not only to repent, but to engage our Christian responsibility to be Patriots even as we proclaim the Gospel in living and speaking.

---

[15]   See the following site for a discussion of three principles to guide the free speech of Christians in the marketplace, including the public schools: [https:/ http://bit.ly/oUu8JX/].

Action Steps:

ACTION STEP 1

Date Completed _____
Outcome

ACTION STEP 2

Date Completed _____
Outcome

ACTION STEP 3

Date Completed _____
Outcome

Week 28   Date: _____
Generational Transference of Blessings
Text: *Deuteronomy 5:29; 6:1–25*

Weekly Reading:
As with Old Testament Israel (Num. 11:4), so with Colonial America: the
population was a mixed multitude (believers and unbelievers). But again,
as with Israel, so also with Colonial America: the majorities were people of
faith. In this week's text from Deuteronomy, God, through Moses, sets forth
a pattern or model for the transference both of the corpus of the people's
faith and the reality of their faith in order to ensure continuance of the
blessings that God bestowed on them from generation to generation. As
twenty-first-century Americans, as well as those who desire to be Christian
Patriots, we must adopt this pattern if we are to pass on the blessings that
God has bestowed on us to the next generation and beyond. Here is the
pattern, to be read from the bottom up:

Focusing on redemption (vv. 20–25)
> When questioned, we need to focus on God's redemptive act.

Consistent modeling (vv. 10–19)
> We need to be a consistent model of worshiping God in all of life.

Display truth artistically (vv. 8–9)
> We need to use symbolism and art to reinforce reality.

Bookending the day (v. 7d)
> We need to model beginning and ending the day with God.

Intentional application opportunity (v. 7c)
> We must intentionally draw out the application to current events.

Casual application frequently (v. 7b)
> We must apply the Word of God in our daily living.

Formal instruction with regularity (v. 7a)
> We must formally teach our children the Word of God.

Communication intentionally (v. 6)
> We must be intentionally interacting with God.

Relationship is vital (v. 5)
    We must have a vital relationship with God.

Theological foundation (v. 4)
    We must begin with a right view of God.

As Christians, we need to know our theological foundations. As Americans and Patriots, we need to know our foundational documents. We need to know our historical foundations. We need to use this knowledge by applying the above model to transfer our appreciation for God's blessings to our national identity. Allow me to give you one example from the above model. I believe we should "bookend the day" by being in the presence of God through prayer. This could include, in our morning prayers, a word of thanksgiving to God for General Washington's humility as he bowed in prayer; in our evening prayers we could offer a word of thanks for Patrick Henry's willingness to take a stand for freedom and cry out, "Give me liberty or give me death!" Throughout the course of the day we need to model Christianity in our families, our churches, and our jobs. Likewise we need to model love for our country.

Prayer:
Gracious God, author of redemption, thank you that you taught Israel how to transfer your blessings from one generation to another. Thank you also for recording both the process and the outcome of their failure to follow your model. You have told us that these things were written for our instruction. Now, Lord God, we see our nation and the blessings you have bestowed on us in jeopardy because we have failed to be instructed by your record of Israel's failure to implement this model. As Daniel of old, Father, we would offer repentance, both for our sins as your church in failing to transfer to succeeding generations a knowledge of who you are and for all you have done to redeem us, and as a nation in failing to transfer an understanding of your providence on our behalf. Grant, Lord, a revival!

Action Steps:

ACTION STEP 1

Date Completed _____
Outcome

ACTION STEP 2

Date Completed _____
Outcome

ACTION STEP 3

Date Completed _____
Outcome

Week 29   Date: _____
Washington's Thanksgiving Proclamation
Text: *Deuteronomy 30:1–20*

Weekly Reading:
This week, we will read the 1789 proclamation by George Washington that
established the holiday of Thanksgiving for our nation. There are no words
I could add to his that would better convey his belief in a Divine Providence
and the need for our nation to constantly and consistently return thanks to
a gracious God who has blessed our nation. Read this and think of where our
nation's leaders are now.

> *Whereas it is the duty of all nations to acknowledge the
> providence of Almighty God, to obey His will, to be grateful
> for His benefits, and humbly to implore His protection and
> favor; and Whereas both Houses of Congress have, by their
> joint committee, requested me to* "recommend to the people
> of the United States a day of public thanksgiving and prayer,
> to be observed by acknowledging with grateful hearts
> the many and signal favors of Almighty God, especially by
> affording them an opportunity peaceably to establish a
> form of government for their safety and happiness."

> *Now, therefore, I do recommend and assign Thursday, the
> 26th day of November next, to be devoted by the people of
> these States to the service of that great and glorious Being
> who is the beneficent author of all the good that was, that
> is, or that will be; that we may then all unite in rendering
> unto Him our sincere and humble thanks for His kind care
> and protection of the people of this country previous to their
> becoming a nation; for the signal and manifold mercies and
> the favorable interpositions of His providence in the course
> and conclusion of the late war; for the great degree of
> tranquility, union, and plenty which we have since enjoyed;
> for the peaceable and rational manner in which we have
> been enabled to establish constitutions of government for
> our safety and happiness, and particularly the national one
> now lately instituted for the civil and religious liberty with
> which we are blessed, and the means we have of acquiring
> and diffusing useful knowledge; and, in general, for all the*

great and various favors which He has been pleased to confer upon us.

And also that we may then unite in most humbly offering our prayers and supplications to the great Lord and Ruler of Nations and beseech Him to pardon our national and other transgressions; to enable us all, whether in public or private stations, to perform our several and relative duties properly and punctually; to render our National Government a blessing to all the people by constantly being a Government of wise, just, and constitutional laws, discreetly and faithfully executed and obeyed; to protect and guide all sovereigns and nations (especially such as have shown kindness to us), and to bless them with good governments, peace, and concord; to promote the knowledge and practice of true religion and virtue, and the increase of science among them and us; and, generally to grant unto all mankind such a degree of temporal prosperity as He alone knows to be best.

Given under my hand, at the city of New York, the 3rd day of October, A.D. 1789.

George Washington, President

Prayer:
O, Lord, as Christian Patriots we can only drop to the knee in humble thanksgiving for the gift of such a leader. Father, give us such a leader again. Grant us such affliction that will press the majority of our people into willingly accepting such leadership. Bring us to the point that we will join the psalmist in crying out, "It was good for me to be afflicted." Grant us, Lord, to become a thankful nation that in humility we will once again proclaim Divine Providence as sovereign in the affairs of men and the Gospel as essential for life.

Action Steps:

ACTION STEP 1

Date Completed _____
Outcome

ACTION STEP 2

Date Completed _____
Outcome

ACTION STEP 3

Date Completed _____
Outcome

Week 30   Date: _____
Ignorance Leads to Confusion
Text: *Deuteronomy 6:4–9*

Weekly Reading:
Tim Kephart,[16] a journalist for a CBS news outlet in Florida, reported on the growing ignorance of American history as illustrated in a survey regarding the Fourth of July. The survey suggested viewing this ignorance through different stratifications of the populace. Perhaps the most alarming statistic is regarding those between the ages of 18 and 29. Forty percent of those polled did not know that America won independence from England. Little wonder that a large percentage of the contemporary population does not realize that the principles of Judeo-Christian ethics and values form the core of our national existence. But even more significant is the fact that they fight against the very idea that history validates as fact.

Ignorance has two sources in America, even as it did in ancient Israel. First, there was a failure of one generation to transfer the truth to the next generation, which we discussed a few weeks ago. The other was a determined effort to displace truth with error in order to gain and maintain control of the populace. God exhorted Israel to establish truth transference in the smallest unit of society, the family. This is delineated in today's text. This most powerful and effective means of transference is dependent on each family's obedience. It also demonstrates the possibility of a slow deterioration of truth, since failure in one family can be overcome by the composite of many other families. However, when failure to be obedient reaches exponential proportions, ignorance prevails and error controls.

In I Kings 12:25–33, Jeroboam not only divided the nation, but he established and fostered error in order to gain and maintain control. The result was disastrous in two ways: First, religious error seeped into every dimension of life, generating a society of elitists who failed to practice justice and mercy. Second, it warped worship into a self-centered idolatry.

The mandate for America is simple. Every family of Christian Patriots must practice the instructions of our text for today so as to transfer truth to the next generation. Every pastor needs to do two things. He needs to model today's text in his own family, and he needs to exhort the men and women of his congregation toward the execution of these instructions. He needs

---

16   http://cbs4.com/watercooler/independence.england.america.2.1785445.html

to teach men how to functionally implement them through godly loving leadership in their families. He needs to teach women how to functionally implement them through both teaching and modeling respect in the manner in which she follows her husband's loving leadership.

An accurate read of American Colonial history will remind us that the colonists, in the vast majority, recognized their dependence on God and expressed this dependence both in public and private prayer. Public prayer was often at the bidding of the body politic and modeled by participation. Prayer was widely supported by the variety of denominational structures from Anglicans to Quakers. In our current atmosphere we will find little support from the body politic for prayer, but surely we can find venues through which the diversity of churches today can promote public and private prayer.

O, Christian Patriot, join your family in prayer! Over the last several weeks we have looked at the patterns God has established to transfer blessings. Study the prayers of the Bible! Engage our God on behalf of our nation that we might continue the legacy for freedom and be the engine of the Gospel to the rest of the world. Teach history so that your children learn from the past. Pray that by learning history they will not repeat its mistakes, but will commit themselves to be godly citizens who promote righteousness in both personal and public life.

Prayer:
We thank you, Father, that you have enlightened us regarding our history. We have been blessed by your multifaceted providence. Help us, Father, to painstakingly teach our children regarding the hand of God in American history. Enable us to capitalize these blessings and leverage them for the sake of the furtherance of the Gospel at home and abroad. Amen.

Action Steps:

ACTION STEP 1

Date Completed _____
Outcome

ACTION STEP 2

Date Completed _____
Outcome

ACTION STEP 3

Date Completed _____
Outcome

Week 31   Date: _____
Erosion by Neglect
Text: *Psalm 119:65–80*[17]

Weekly Reading:
When King Solomon died, his son Rehoboam succeeded him. Unfortunately, the later life of Solomon was characterized by his drifting toward idolatry to please his foreign wives. In addition, he violated the injunctions that God gave to kings. In the *founding documents* of Israel, kings were forbidden to engage exploit their power. There were three specific prohibitions:

1.   The prohibition against marrying many wives.
2.   The prohibition against accumulating many horses.
3.   The prohibition against amassing too much silver and gold.

During Solomon's reign, Israel became a wealthy and powerful nation. While the king as well as the population experienced the good life, there were problems. As Rehoboam came to power we observe one of these problems. Jeroboam leads a contingency that appeals to Rehoboam to relieve them of the tax burden imposed by Solomon. Rehoboam does not listen to the seasoned advisors but acts on the advice of his peers and increases taxes. The ten northern tribes join Jeroboam in revolt. Conditions had been slowly advancing toward this revolt. Solomon had become a powerful king. His success allowed him to slowly impose more and more demands on his people as well as publicly engage in idolatry.

Demise is seldom abrupt. It is almost always a creeping sickness. In 2011, the US Department of Justice replaced traditional patriotic symbols with a stark black-and-white format on their website. In addition, rather than using a quote from a Founding Father as a byline, they chose this statement by C. Wilfred Jenks: "The common law is the will of mankind, issuing from the life of the people." Jenks, an activist from the 1930s, participated in the United Nations International Labor Organization and was influential in the development of the Declaration on Social Justice for a Fair Globalization. This document ultimately erodes national law in the United States in favor of international law. It is more than ironic that his quote is used by those revising the US Department of Justice website.

---

[17]   For the historical background concerning this Psalm, see I Kings 12.

God's law for Israel was its foundational framework as a nation. God instructed the leaders to have the entire law read to Israel every seven years in a public forum. Not only was this important tradition ignored, but, as is seen in the case study of Solomon, various dimensions of the law were eroded. In America we have failed to read the Constitution and other founding documents as a population. The result has been the eroding of the intent and genius of these documents with which God gifted this country. If we are to see a religious, political and social revival in our nation we must return to the regular reading of the Word of God and the founding documents of our country. In the passage from Psalm 119 for today there are several themes. One theme regarding God's direct involvement in society and individual life, the affliction of the psalmist, is rather startling. The psalmist writes, "Before I was afflicted I went astray, but now I keep your word . . . . In faithfulness you have afflicted me." How foolish for us as individuals, and as a nation, to drift from God's blessings so that He must afflict us in order to rekindle our appreciation for those same blessings! How much wiser is another theme in this passage that calls us to pray and search for discernment (v. 66) and understanding (v. 73) from His commandments!

Prayer:

O Lord, according to your Word, teach me discernment and grant to me understanding that I might live by your commandments and value the blessings you have given me in my heritage as an American. Lord, thank you for your faithfulness that afflicts me and drives me back to your commandments, your statutes, your Word. May my heart be blameless so that I may never be ashamed!

Action Steps:

ACTION STEP 1

Date Completed _____
Outcome

ACTION STEP 2

Date Completed _____
Outcome

ACTION STEP 3

Date Completed _____
Outcome

Week 32   Date: _____
Every Nation Needs a King
Text: *Judges 17*

Weekly Reading:
People will always have differences, and need a final arbitrator. Our forefathers resisted the push to create a monarchy after the American Revolution. One group of Army officers threatened to remove themselves west to set up a monarchy, but General Washington foiled this movement. There were others who wanted the general to become king of the new nation. We are all grateful that these efforts failed. However, despite their resistance to a monarchy, our forefathers understood that we do need a king, an ultimate authority. That is why they fashioned the Constitution and the Bill of Rights. The law became king for America.

Following Joshua's conquest of the Promised Land, Israel spiraled downward into chaos. The history is recorded for us in the book of Judges. Beginning in 17:6 there is a recurring theme: "In those days there was no king in Israel." This seventeenth chapter records a story that epitomizes the situation in Israel.

In this story we can observe complete disregard for the Ten Commandments, the core of Old Testament law. There is a son, Micah, who dishonored his mother by stealing from her. There is a mother who utters a curse toward the thief and blesses a son who turns out to be the thief, upon his admission to the crime. This same mother rewards this son by giving the returned money to a metalsmith to create an idol for him. The community had drifted so far from God's standards that an idol manufacturer was openly operating.

Idol in hand, Micah consecrates one of his sons to become his priest; but wanting a priest that had a little more credibility in Israel, Micah took in a young man from Bethlehem in Judah, a Levite, and consecrated him the priest of his home. The young man became a priest for hire, being paid a stipend to serve Micah. Micah creates a bastard religion but has so little understanding of God's law that he concludes, "Now I know that the Lord will prosper me, seeing I have a Levite as priest."

Little wonder the last verse of the book of Judges says, "In those days there was no king in Israel; everyone did what was right in his own eyes."

How did Israel sink into this morass of confusion? The answer is simple. Every Israelite was a sinner by nature, including all leaders—even Moses and Joshua who led them out of Egypt and into the Promised Land. They were all desperately in need of practicing the command of Joshua 1:8 that called for perpetual meditation on the book of the law.

The book of the law, the Word of God, was to be king. As leaders and people they needed constant exposure to the Word of God in order not to spiral into the aphorism that *every man was doing what was right in his own eyes*. Our forefathers understood that we needed a king. We simply could not leave our destiny in the hands of political leaders. There had to be an ultimate authority. In America, that ultimate authority is our Constitution and Bill of Rights. These documents established power bases to balance each other and thereby control leaders and citizens from the reign of anarchy— every man doing that which is right in his own eyes.

In God's providence we, as Christian Patriots, have the Constitution and the Bill of Rights, which honor the principles of God's Word to guide our leaders and citizens—whether believers or not. As Christians we have God's Word to guide and control our lives, both as citizens of the Kingdom of God and citizens of America. In both cases embracing and meditating on these documents is the only thing that will reverse the current drift in the church and the country toward *every man doing that which is right in his own eyes.*

Prayer:
Almighty God, author of the Word of God and granter of our founding documents, enable our people to understand the absolute necessity to be ever focused on these documents. Your Word is the expression of your will as King of the church. Our founding documents are the expressed authority (king) that provides the anchor for our nation. Forgive us for our tendency to abandon both, and enable us to repent.

Action Steps:

ACTION STEP 1

Date Completed _____
Outcome

ACTION STEP 2

Date Completed _____
Outcome

ACTION STEP 3

Date Completed _____
Outcome

Week 33   Date: _____
Commemoratives: What are They Worth?
Text: *Joshua 4*

Weekly Reading:
Travel to Philadelphia and Washington and you will see many memorials to remind us of God's hand on this nation and its leaders. Unfortunately, for the majority of the population these memorials are museum pieces. When I was a boy growing up in Pennsylvania, we took school trips to both cities. We were herded in groups of 40 to 50 from one monument to another with but rudimentary instruction as to their meaning.

The generation of Israel that experienced the extraordinary work of God to win their release from 400 years of Egyptian slavery failed to believe that God could enable them to take the Promised Land. As a result, that generation died off during the 40 years of wilderness wandering. God transfers leadership to Joshua through His first act of orchestrating the Israelites' crossing of the Jordan River (Joshua 4:14).

God parts the waters of the Jordan so that "all Israel crossed on dry ground" (3:17). There are at least two miracles here. One is that the waters are held back apparently without flooding, and the second is that the ground in the riverbed immediately became dry ground—their sandals did not even get muddy. As the crossing is coming to an end, God calls Joshua aside for a conference (4:1–3) and instructs him to send twelve men, one from each tribe, back into the river to retrieve a sizable stone to be used in building a memorial (4:21–23).

This memorial, this *ebenezer*, has two purposes. Joshua instructs the people that the first purpose is evangelistic. Joshua puts it this way, "That all peoples of the earth may know that the hand of the Lord is mighty." God was using Israel to showcase himself so that all peoples would be drawn to him. The second purpose was to remind Israel to "Fear the Lord your God forever" (4:24).

But memorials only achieve their purpose if each generation does two things. First, each generation must live the faith that the ebenezer memorializes. If they don't live it, the memorial becomes a museum piece. Second, each generation must instruct the next generation by telling the story behind the memorial in order to invest it with life and meaning. Most of the memorials of Israel became functionaries for the vast majority of the people. On occasion, in the midst of a revival, the memorials took on life for a short time. God's intention for the memorials is clear, but the people's lack of execution devalued them.

The breakdown in Israel was at the family level. Note that Joshua says, "When your children ask their fathers" (Joshua 4:21). It was the responsibility of individual fathers, the parents, to teach individual children about the work of God that the memorial represented. Fathers have failed in America. To a large degree fathers have depended on the church to teach their children who God is and what God has done. In the same manner, fathers have depended on the schools to teach the meaning of the memorials of American history. As a result, our children grow up with very little appreciation for the unique hand of God in the lives and actions of our Founding Fathers. So, once again, we see that the model God provides in the Bible in the life of Israel is instructive for us as Christian Patriots. Will we learn from their failure to capitalize on God's model?

Prayer:
Father, you have informed us that the records of Israel have been written for our instruction. Help us both in the conveyance of our faith and the transferring of our national heritage to take responsibility as fathers and parents both to live with vitality and teach with intentionality. Grant, O Lord, a revival in your church and in our nation.

Action Steps:

ACTION STEP 1

Date Completed _____
Outcome

ACTION STEP 2

Date Completed _____
Outcome

ACTION STEP 3

Date Completed _____
Outcome

Week 34   Date: _____
Contemplating Religion, Clarity, and Compromise
Text: *Joshua 9*

Weekly Reading:
We have, over the past few weeks, been looking closely at Joshua and the Judges of Israel. In this week's passage, Joshua was tricked into compromising with a pagan people. It requires no small leap of the imagination to believe that we, as a nation and a church, are being tempted to fall into a similar compromise.

In the year of this book's authorship, 2011, the political scene in America is a bit reminiscent of the era of King James I of England. Between 1603 (the beginning of the reign of James I) and 1625 (the coronation of Charles I), there was a growing unrest in England. King James was interested in Christianity not so much for its religious value as for its political power. King James attempted to contain the Puritans by agreeing to a new translation of the Bible, the King James Version, in exchange for their embracing of the practices of the Church of England. He was so determined to achieve his ends that it is said he proclaimed, "I will make them conform themselves, or I will harry them out of the land." It reminds one of the 2010 presidential policies regarding the purchase of health-care insurance.

These tensions intensified under Charles I. As titular head of the Church of England he was able to place as Archbishop of Canterbury William Laud, who was bent on restoring Catholic elements to the Anglican Church. It is true that Laud may have had a religious agenda, but King Charles, like James I, used the church for his own political desires. Laud demanded that Puritans fully comply with Anglican worship forms. When the Puritans refused, various forms of persecution ensued.

In contemporary England and America we are witnessing a growing alliance between state governments and Islam. This can be observed in preferential treatment for Islamic interests. One example is the establishment of *sharia* law (the sacred law of Islam) as parallel to civil law in some European countries. Currently there are five *sharia* courts in England. Islamic banking institutions exist in other Western nations such as Denmark, France, Germany, Netherlands, and Switzerland.

I believe that Islam in America is beginning to take on the political role of the Anglican Church in the reign of Charles I. We are all familiar with the Islamic army major responsible for the shootings at Fort Hood in Texas. Army officials admit to being concerned about him but being unwilling to take action to secure him for fear of the Islamic backlash. Another example is police Capt. Paul Fields of Tulsa, who was relieved of duty for being unwilling to attend an Islamic-sponsored event in his city.[18]

During the seventeenth century, the Puritans and the king found an option. The Puritans had clarity. They envisioned America as a place where they could worship God as they biblically believed and where they could set up a government based on the Bible. The king was glad to be rid of them and agreed to charter the Massachusetts Bay Colony. Thus in God's providence, a sophisticated theological foundation was laid for American freedom and self-government. Unlike those who settled Jamestown, these Puritans, who came by the tens of thousands between 1630 and 1660, shared a cohesive Judeo-Christian worldview. Their constituency was solidly educated tradesmen, merchants, and professionals. They possessed the theological foundation and the practical acumen to fashion a nation.

It is now our turn! As Christian Patriots we hold the product that their embryonic work produced. We have a Constitution and a Bill of Rights. We have religious freedom. Let us not sacrifice freedom on the altar of so-called toleration! We must proclaim liberty from sin through Jesus Christ. We must proclaim liberty from tyranny by both exercising our right to self-government and teaching our contemporaries and our children the values of the Judeo-Christian foundation on which we stand.

Prayer:
Almighty God, you, who by your providence have worked through history to give us both religious and political freedom, enable us to stand firm on our foundation. Enable us to proclaim liberty from the slavery of sin through the redemptive work of our Lord Jesus Christ. And enable us not to take pride in being Americans, but in humility proclaim the great God-given privileges you have been pleased to establish in this nation and through which you have been pleased to bless much of the world with your Gospel. Protect our leaders from leading us into compromise with cultural and religious demands lest we encumber ourselves with such alliances.

---

[18]   Jonathan M. Seidl. "Oklahoma Police Captain Transferred". http://bit.ly/qtvKQX

Action Steps:

ACTION STEP 1

Date Completed _____
Outcome

ACTION STEP 2

Date Completed _____
Outcome

ACTION STEP 3

Date Completed _____
Outcome

Week 35   Date: _____
Determine Direction by Principle, Not by Experience
Text: *Deuteronomy 13:1–4*

Weekly Reading:
Over and over again, throughout the Pentateuch, Israel is challenged to listen to the Word of God and not their immediate desires. In this passage Moses makes a very pointed application of this principle. Even if a prophet shows up with a prophecy that comes true, don't trust the experience of prophecy over the Word of God. This is not a problem confined to the early Israelites.

When I was a young man, there was a prophetess in America by the name of Jeane Dixon. She had a surprising ability to couch her prophecies in such a manner that a certain percentage of them could be considered fulfilled. She gained a good bit of press and garnered a following. But wagering one's life, religious or otherwise, on her experience of "being right" would have been foolhardy.

Christians must always be on guard not to substitute experience in the form of feelings or desires for the clear teaching of the Word of God. It behooves the Christian to understand the Word of God in terms of its historical setting. The documents of Scripture, its concepts and words, must be interpreted in their historical context. The grammatical structure must be understood in the historical context. For example, this passage instructs Israel to execute false prophets who would entice them to follow false gods and enter into the idolatry of the peoples among whom they dwelt. Unless this passage is understood in the historical context of the theocracy of Israel, the modern Christian could conceivably call for the stoning of Jeane Dixon. Instead, the modern Christian must interpret the passage in the historical context and extract from it the principle embedded in the historical framework. So Paul writes in I Corinthians 10, "These things were written for our instruction."

All interpretation, then, must flow from a grammatical-historical understanding of a given passage. The Constitution and the Bill of Rights can only be properly interpreted by utilizing these same principles. The historical context is the framework. The grammatical construction and the meaning of words and concepts must be understood in terms of the intellectual, social, and political climate. This is the only way in which we can adequately appreciate the intent of our forefathers. Likewise, it is imperative to acknowledge the theological environment. For example, it is essential to comprehend that the God of the Bible is the Providence about which men such as George Washington spoke.[19] In order for our nation to maintain the integrity as conceived by our forefathers, contemporary issues must be addressed through these lenses.

Today we are inundated by *prophets* who would ignore at best, and trash at worst, these documents on which we stand and their theological foundation: the Word of God. If we are to survive and pass on to our children and grandchildren the wonderful gift of freedom bestowed on us by a gracious God for the furtherance of His kingdom through the spread of the Gospel, then we must take up the responsibility both to live obediently to the Word and to guard what has been delivered to us as a nation.

Prayer:
Gracious Father in heaven who has graced us with the knowledge of the redeeming blood of Jesus Christ that purchased our salvation, grant us the wisdom to discern the false prophets in our midst as they would attempt to entice us into following the false gods of our age. Grant us also the determination to guard what you have delivered to us—the Word of God and a nation grounded in the theological foundation of your Word.

---

[19]   See *Sacred Fire* by Peter Lillback for an in-depth discussion of this matter.

Action Steps:

ACTION STEP 1

Date Completed _____
Outcome

ACTION STEP 2

Date Completed _____
Outcome

ACTION STEP 3

Date Completed _____
Outcome

Week 36   Date: _____
Dual Citizenship
Text: *Hebrews 12*

Weekly Reading:
I have the opportunity to sing many wonderful classic and new classic Christian hymns in my weekly worship with the body of Christ. The opening lines of a familiar Christian song run like this:

> *This world is not my home . . . I'm just 'a passing through*
> *My treasures are laid up . . . somewhere beyond the blue.*[20]

One thing Christian Patriots always have to remember is that they have dual citizenship. Our American citizenship will end. Our citizenship in God's kingdom will not. Therefore, our American citizenship must be executed in the framework of our citizenship in the Kingdom of God.

This concept is not new. It pervades the Bible. Abraham, to whom God made a covenant to proliferate his seed as the sand of the seashore (Genesis 12 and 17), lived out his existence as a nomad. The writer of Hebrews tells us, however, that Abraham looked for a city with foundations, whose builder and maker is God (11:10). As one writer said it, "He looked for a city and lived in a tent!" He had a dual citizenship.

Jesus articulates this reality in his encounter with Nicodemus. Nicodemus's curiosity piqued and he decided to risk a personal investigation of Jesus. Being a high-ranking official in the Jewish structure, he did not want to hazard being caught in a public one-on-one with Jesus. Jesus goes immediately to the heart of the issue. Nicodemus must have a second citizenship in order to participate in the Kingdom of God. In essence, Jesus explains that Nicodemus has a natural passport through being born of water. That is, Nicodemus has been physically born into Israel. However, in order to enter the Kingdom of God, he must be born again by the Spirit. He needed a heavenly citizenship and he could only get it by being birthed into the kingdom. He, too, needed dual citizenship.

America is where God has placed us. We were born here and thereby obtained citizenship. We have been born again by the Spirit and thereby

---

[20]   Musicnotes.com . E.B. Graham. Digital Sheet Music. [There are a bewildering number of references to the possible origin of this song.

issued citizenship in the Kingdom of God. John put it this way, "But as many as received Him, to them He gave the right to become children of God . . . were not born . . . of the will of man, but of God" (John 1:12). That we are citizens of heaven dictates that we should be grateful to be Americans and engaged in maintaining the blessings.

In the twelfth chapter of Hebrews, the author challenges believers in light of the great cloud of witnesses listed in chapter 11—including Abraham, who lived as an alien while looking for the city that God designed—to run with endurance the race that is set before us (Heb. 12:1). He gives us three ways to practice kingdom citizenship that will contribute to our endurance and will impact our earthly citizenship at the same time. First, in 12:2, we are to fix our eyes on Jesus—who "for the joy set before him *endured* . . . ." We draw our strength both from the model of Jesus and the power of Jesus (Matt. 28:18). Second, we are to pursue peace and holiness (12:14). Third, we are to live our earthly citizenship as kingdom citizens (12:28). We are Christian Patriots, citizens in two worlds—but one of those citizenships is eternal. We must live like it!

Prayer:
Almighty God, giver of earthly and heavenly citizenships, help us to live out our earthly citizenship in light of the reality of our heavenly citizenship. As Christian Patriots, enable us to see to it that we do not come short of Your grace; that we allow no root of bitterness to spring up since it will defile many. Lord, it is so easy in our American citizenship to become bitter toward our leaders who abandon the good gifts you secured through our forefathers and in the process tarnish our heavenly citizenship. Help us, Lord, to pray for them and work to elect those who will honor your gifts. Do not let us tarnish our heavenly citizenship; rather, let our citizenship in your kingdom cause our citizenship in America to shine for you.

Action Steps:

ACTION STEP 1

Date Completed _____
Outcome

ACTION STEP 2

Date Completed _____
Outcome

ACTION STEP 3

Date Completed _____
Outcome

Week 37 Date: _____
Choosing Leadership is Serious Business
Text: *Acts 6:1–6* and *I Timothy 3:1–13*

Weekly Reading:
In Acts 20: 29–30 the apostle Paul warns the elders at Ephesus that the church would come under attack from two sources, outside the church and inside the church. The opposition from inside the church would come from leaders "speaking perverse things, to draw away the disciples after them."

The two passages for our meditation today focus on the philosophy and the methods of choosing leadership in the church. The two methods we observe are appointment (Titus 1:5) and election (Acts 6:3). In either case the philosophy embodied in the process is extremely instructive. Notice that in both cases belief, character, and the conduct of life are important. That is, does the candidate live the ideals that are embodied in the Word of God?

There is also a second dimension of concern: do the elected officials represent the ethnic complexity of the congregation? The picture of the clash between the Jewish congregants and the Greek congregants in Acts 6 can be observed over and over again in history. Only the names of the players change. The apostles brilliantly adopted a means to minimize the problem. They introduced diversity in the leadership. Such wise procedures on behalf of the apostles did not lead to a trouble-free church, as history attests. In reality, as a body instituted by God but made up of fallen human beings, the church historically did not do a very good job of implementing these wise precautions and, in the process, left us a rather colorful, convoluted, and sometimes sinful record.

The principle, however, is the same. Our Founding Fathers provided parallel standards for public officials. They even took heed to Paul's caution not to place in leadership a new convert; that is, one with little experience. At a time in history when the average life span was 47 years, one had to be 35 years of age to quality for the presidency. That is, on the average, to be presidential one had to have lived out 66 percent of his life.

Overall, our Founding Fathers set parameters that humanly ensured that those who followed them were similar in belief, character, and manner of life. They understood that if the next generation was going to protect and perfect the nation for which they had risked their fortunes and lives, there must be set common standards as well as a common responsibility to perpetuate the intellectual and moral fabric of America.

So once again we find a great deal of correspondence between our Christian life and our national life. We should not be surprised since our Founding Fathers drew heavily on our Christian foundation. As a Christian Patriot today, you find yourself (as I do) in a culture that is eroding both the intellectual and the moral fabric of church and state. As God through Paul exhorted the elders at Ephesus, so he exhorts us. *Be on guard* for yourselves and for all the flock—for both the church and the nation. There are those within and without who would destroy the church for which Jesus shed his blood. In the same way, there are those within and without who would destroy the nation that God has given us through our Founding Fathers, building on the good Word of God. A significant way in which we guard both the church and nation is by exercising our responsibility to be discerning of those who run for office and then participate in the election process.

Prayer:
Lord, you have called us to accountability. You have instructed us as to how we can be involved in sustaining a vibrant, serving church and a nation in which we flourish, and thereby promote your kingdom worldwide. Lord, grant us the wisdom to discern godly leaders and determination to participate in our civil and church responsibilities.

Action Steps:

ACTION STEP 1

Date Completed _____
Outcome

ACTION STEP 2

Date Completed _____
Outcome

ACTION STEP 3

Date Completed _____
Outcome

Week 38   Date: _____
Celebrating the Infancy of Self-Government under God
Text: *Deuteronomy 16:18–20*

Weekly Reading:
The Virginia House of Burgesses, which was to become known as the General Assembly, is the oldest legislative body in the Western Hemisphere. The initial meeting of this body was on July 30, 1619. This meeting was opened in prayer by the Reverend Richard Bucke. A Jamestown official expressed the sentiment of the Burgesses when he observed regarding the opening of the meeting in prayer that "men's affaires doe little prosper where Gods service is neglected."[21] God graciously blessed these infant efforts toward self-government by having the work of the Virginia House of Burgesses ratified in 1621.

There are many today who would deny that the concept of freedom espoused by our Founding Fathers has its basis in the Bible. One writer observed, "Despite being regularly described as Christian or biblical in American rhetoric, freedom is not a concept the Bible is familiar with (and the biblical warrant for democracy is even smaller)."[22] Apparently he has not read the passage for our consideration today.

There were two dimensions to the concept of freedom laid out by our founders. One concept was that of political freedom. It was the right of self-government. As our passage demonstrates, Israel, a theocracy, was responsible for self-governing. The second dimension of freedom was the manner in which one worshiped. Unfortunately, clarifying the meaning and practice of freedom in the matter of worship has been a difficult and convoluted endeavor. The early history of New England and New York leaves no question regarding the struggle for religious freedom for Roman Catholics and Baptists. That this struggle continued in modern America was evident when John F. Kennedy ran for president. The fact that he was Roman Catholic became a political liability. More recently, Republican presidential hopeful Mitt Romney's Mormonism caused a similar stir in the 2008 and 2012 presidential primaries.

---

[21]   Journals of the House of Burgesses of Virginia. Cited on Google March 13, 2011.

[22]   Clifford Longley, *Global Dialogue*, Volume 5, Number 1–2. Winter/Spring 2003.

However, these issues do not suggest that we despise the good gifts of political and religious freedom that God has graciously bestowed on us. Like Daniel, we should offer prayers of repentance where our Founding Fathers—and we—have sinned and failed. We should return to the Word of God for instruction, wisdom, and understanding. As we do, we are reminded that religious freedom is first of all the freedom that Christ has provided. We are freed from sin (Rom. 6:7) to present ourselves as living and holy sacrifices to God, which is our spiritual service of worship (Rom. 12:1).

Katharine Lee Bates captured the sentiment that should be the national prayer of every Christian Patriot when she wrote:

> America! America!
> God mend thine ev'ry flaw,
> Confirm thy soul in self-control,
> Thy liberty in law.

Bates understood America. She appreciated that our history and our founding documents are steeped in the God of the Bible, but that we are flawed by our sinful bent. Therefore her poem is a perpetual prayer for Divine intervention, both to correct our flaws and to exercise the self-control that can continually refine our liberty within the framework of law.

Prayer:
Merciful God of heaven, the giver of every good gift, shed your grace on our nation. Grant that we would recognize every citizen as a fellow heir to the benefits with which you have endowed this nation. Grant that we should be found engaged in guarding, refining, and expanding the freedom embedded in our founding documents. And Father, most of all, let us be found trumpeting the Gospel that proclaims freedom from the slavery of sin. Protect our nation, Lord, so it might continue to be a strong base of operations for the Kingdom of God.

Action Steps:

ACTION STEP 1

Date Completed _____
Outcome

ACTION STEP 2

Date Completed _____
Outcome

ACTION STEP 3

Date Completed _____
Outcome

Week 39   Date: _____
American Principles and Practices Are Rooted in God
Text: *Deuteronomy 23:9–25*

Weekly Reading:
The establishment of a nation is a difficult task. Mao Tse-tung gained power
in 1949 in China. By 1966 he laid out a blueprint for the reestablishment of
China in the *Little Red Book*. Carrying a copy of this manual became virtually
mandatory for a Communist Party member, in China and around the world.
Mao portrayed himself as a god, as evidenced by the cult personality that
developed around him. Another popular communist leader of the twentieth
century, Vladimir Lenin, laid out a plan for the reestablishment of Russia
as the USSR. He penned fifty-four volumes, each about 650 pages. In his
collected writings, Lenin refined the ideas Karl Marx expressed in *The
Communist Manifesto*. In the classical world, Alexander the Great had a
pattern by which he incorporated conquered lands into his kingdom. But
all of these attempts at kingdom building across history lacked a principled
moral framework out of which a country could develop a course of self-
correcting that strived to create an environment that benefited everyone.
For Mao and Lenin, equality meant economic sameness. Freedom meant
socialism. For Alexander the Great, inclusion meant subjugation. Freedom
was power.

How different was the American experiment! There was not one leader
who imagined what America should be. There was no proletarian revolution
of the working class seeking to better their lot in life. There was no desire
to place one ruling group over another. The American experiment began,
for the most part, with congregations of believers banding together to seek
a place in the New World to establish a structure that would allow them
to worship as they believed the Bible commanded. Paralleling these groups
of believers were the economic companies willing to invest in the New
World for capitalist gains and free market expansion. Even these companies,
however, sought the expansion of the Kingdom of God and provided for a
biblical expression of worship.

Yet America was not the new Israel. America was not the Promised Land
replacement, a manmade New Jerusalem. America was a nation founded
on a plethora of principles that formed its core values extracted from God's
instructions to ancient Israel.

The passage before us today provides us an example. The conduct of an army is prescribed. "You shall keep yourself from every evil thing" (v. 9). This has characterized the American military, and when this principle has been violated there have been disciplinary consequences. The principle of good sanitary practices can be drawn from verses 10–14. The principle of political asylum can be drawn from verses 15–16. The principle of charging appropriate interest in business can be seen in verse 20. The societal responsibility for provision of a means by which the poor among us can provide for themselves is seen in verses 24–25.

The Bible and the God of the Bible are at the core of America. Our cuntry became a great nation because its core values enabled her to capitalize on its almost endless resources in a governmental context of freedom, both politically and religiously. As Christian Patriots we must lead the way toward a reaffirmation of those core values that were biblically framed and rooted. We must live, teach, and preach these values, and we must carefully appraise those we elect by these values.

Prayer:
Father, for your leading of our forefathers to develop a philosophy (a system of core values) that emanates from your character revealed in the Old and New Testaments, we give you thanks. For a free society in which our people can worship you without reprisal, we give you thanks. For a free society in which our people can thrive, we give you thanks. Yet, Lord, we would plead with you for a revival among our people as we observe the erosion of this philosophy that has turned us off course. Deliver us, please, from our diversions, lest we self-destruct, being overcome by evil. Amen.

Action Steps:

ACTION STEP 1

Date Completed _____

Outcome

ACTION STEP 2

Date Completed _____

Outcome

ACTION STEP 3

Date Completed _____

Outcome

Week 40   Date: _____
A Return to Our Roots
Text: *2 Kings 19:14–19*

Weekly Reading:
On March 20, 1779, as governor of Massachusetts, Samuel Adams issued a proclamation calling for a "Day of Solemn Fasting and Prayer." In part, the proclamation called on the citizens, ". . . humbly beseeching God to imbue us with all Christian spirit of Piety, Benevolence and Love of our Country; and that in all public deliberations we may be possessed of a sacred regard to the fundamental principles of our free elective civil Constitutions . . . ." In his concluding paragraph he wrote, "I concede that we cannot better express ourselves than by humbly supplicating the Supreme Ruler of the World."[23] This is but one example of a recurring theme of our forefathers' recognition of our need for humility, repentance, and dependence on the Almighty God.[24]

These are the words of an American Patriot who greatly influenced the shaping of America's founding documents, thereby framing the contours of this nation and ensuring freedom from tyranny while, at the same time, casting a vision of freedom. For certain, greed and avarice have caused us to stumble; yet the foundation and vision infused by knowledge of Providence has thus far preserved our individual and national freedom.

The threat to American liberty came from without. England was going back on the charters that granted various levels of freedom to the colonists, while at the same time imposing taxes without representation from the people. The threat to American liberty today comes from foreign sources that advocate the idols of socialism and elitism. These have gradually marinated into the political fabric of America.

The call of Gov. Adams issued in the midst of the American Revolution is valid for us today. The power of the call comes not from this historical document, but rather from the sacred model repeated in numerous ways in the Word of God. One of those models is the prayer of Hezekiah, found in 2 Kings 19. At its essence, Hezekiah prays that as God has demonstrated previously that idols cannot stand, so now God, "save us, please . . . that all the kingdoms of the earth may know that you, O Lord, are God alone."

---

[23]   http://www.shadesofgrace.org/2010/05/04/americas-founders-proclamations-for-fasting-and-prayer/.
[24]   http://www.john-uebersax.com/plato/proclam.htm This site provides an array of resources citing such documents from Washington to Bush.

As Christians who are Patriots, our desire for God's hand on our nation should first of all be that all the kingdoms of the earth would know that the Lord, our God, is God alone. Yes, we should desire that our leaders would reaffirm the gift of freedom and the foundational documents that birthed and support that freedom. But if our prayer is simply rooted in our selfish desire to preserve our wealth and personal freedom in order to revel in our pleasures, then freedom has become an idol that will bring a curse on us. As Christian Patriots our personal enjoyment must be the outflow of the greater good of the glory of God and the advancement of His kingdom.

Hezekiah found himself and his people outnumbered and outgunned. He turned to an arsenal that the forces of evil cannot foil. So, fellow patriot, we are outnumbered but we are not outgunned, for we have access to an arsenal that cannot be foiled. Let us humble ourselves and turn to God to bring about the second American Revolution, revolution for Christ, by using the rights of voting secured for us by God through our forefathers in the first American Revolution.

Prayer:
The 1928 Book of Common Prayer captures this sentiment in the following Prayer: "Most gracious God, we humbly beseech thee, as for the people of these United States in general, so especially for their Senate and Representatives in Congress assembled; that thou wouldest be pleased to direct and prosper all their consultations, to the advancement of thy glory, the good of thy Church, the safety, honour, and welfare of thy people; that all things may be so ordered and settled by their endeavours, upon the best and surest foundations, that peace and happiness, truth and justice, religion and piety, may be established among us for all generations. These and all other necessaries, for them, for us, and thy whole Church, we humbly beg in the Name and mediation of Jesus Christ, our most blessed Lord and Saviour. Amen."

Action Steps:

ACTION STEP 1

Date Completed _____
Outcome

ACTION STEP 2

Date Completed _____
Outcome

ACTION STEP 3

Date Completed _____
Outcome

Week 41   Date: _____
A Warning for the Church Is a Warning for America
Text: *2 Peter 2:1–3a, Matthew 24:23–27*

Weekly Reading:
As Christian Patriots we find ourselves in a double bind. The very essence of our reality is under a full frontal attack. In the last century, under the influence of modernism, the reality of truth was accepted but a religious approach was isolated by a science that relegated faith to an irrational leap. In contemporary society, truth has been relegated to absolute relativism—that is, nonexistent. Hence, addressing this type of society with the challenge of the truth of God is considered to be nonsense. Of course, did not Paul tell us that "the preaching of the cross is foolishness"? Addressing our fellow citizens with the truth of our founding documents and the teachings of our Founding Fathers is likewise foolishness in an age of relativism and narcissism.

A warning that runs throughout both the Old and the New Testaments is an alert to be on the lookout for false prophets. This warning makes the assumption that there is truth. If there is no truth, no right, no standard, then there cannot be false prophets. But the warning to be alert for false prophets affirms there is truth from which they depart.

There are three simple tests that enable us to identify a false prophet—or teacher—in the church. These tests come in the form of questions. First, "What does this individual say about Jesus?" There are three passages that support this question: Matthew 16:15–16, 2 John 9, and I John 2:22. The second question is, "Does this prophet preach the Gospel?" Again, there are three key passages in support of this question: I Corinthians 15:1–4, Galatians 1:7, and Galatians 1:9. The third question requires our observance of the life of the teacher. "Does this prophet exhibit character qualities that glorify the Lord?" Jude 11 and Matthew 7:15–20 discuss this in some detail. One Bible teacher from the mid-twentieth century put it this way, "Does he walk the talk?"

A study of the New Testament records shows that the early church, and the church history that follows, is replete with accounts of the struggles with false prophets. For example, Paul warns the elders of the church at Ephesus that there would arise from without and from within the church "savage wolves . . . speaking perverse things to draw away the disciples after them"

(Acts 20:27–30). Paul addresses the Judaizers in the book of Galatians. He challenges Timothy to guard the Gospel and to "instruct certain men not to teach strange doctrines" (I Timothy 1:3). Again to Timothy, Paul enjoins the church to "retain the standard of sound words" (2 Timothy 2:13). Titus is warned that "there are many rebellious men, empty talkers and deceivers, especially those of the circumcision" (Titus 1:10). Peter and Jude join Paul in exhorting the church to beware of false prophets and teachers.

Old Testament Israel was born out of a world of raw paganism. New Testament Christianity was born in the cradle of false religion where flagrant idolatry was everywhere. Prophets, magicians, and intellectual defenders of paganism flourished. The reaction to those in society who do not want to hear the truth regarding morality, the sanctity of marriage and the viability of a child in the womb is rapidly approaching the time of the apostle Paul. Their conviction generated sufficient rage to lead to the persecution and stoning of Stephen. Perhaps in no time since the early church has society been so similar to that period of history. Truth is challenged everywhere, from the street thug to the halls of the university. The church finds many within its own walls purveying false doctrines such as universalism and biblical relativism. We should not then be surprised that truth in the political realm has become elusive and, for the mass of society, impossible to discern and or tolerate. Persecution is already evident and will only become uglier.

Yet we must not cease to challenge false prophets in the church or in our nation. The Christian Patriot must continue in the tradition of the apostles and in the tradition of our forefathers. We must live with a faith that trusts that God is there; or, as Francis Schaeffer put it in the title of a book, *He is There and He is Not Silent*. Our faith demands our faithfulness and our faith reassures us that whether or not repentance and revitalization occur in the church or the nation, we win because Jesus is coming again to establish his Kingdom forever and ever. We must live with the confidence of the groundskeeper who, when questioned what he was reading, replied, "The book of Revelation." When asked if he understood what he was reading, he replied, "Yes. Jesus wins!"

Prayer:
Even so come quickly Lord Jesus! But in the meantime, Lord, enable us to be faithful in defending of the truth both in the church and in our civil life. May the good news of the Gospel be heard from our lips, seen in our walk, and reflected in the execution of our personal and civil responsibilities.

Action Steps:

ACTION STEP 1

Date Completed _____
Outcome

ACTION STEP 2

Date Completed _____
Outcome

ACTION STEP 3

Date Completed _____
Outcome

Week 42   Date: _____
A Memorial or a Pile of Stones?
Text: *Joshua 4 and 5*

Weekly Reading:
A short time ago, we looked at the idea of *commemoratives* in the Old
Testament. These are monuments that were put in place by the people of
God to commemorate an event or moment of redemptive history in the life
of Israel. I would like to return to that idea for this week. In our text, Joshua
establishes a memorial. There are different opinions among commentators
as to whether there was one (Joshua 4:3) or two stone memorials (4:9).[25] It
appears that God tells Joshua to put a memorial at the place they lodged,
Gilgal (4:8), and then Joshua had a second memorial set up in the river (4:9).
The purpose of these memorials is fivefold:

1. To provoke their children to ask, "What are these stones?" (4:6, 21)
2. To provide an occasion to instruct children regarding the miracle of
    crossing the Jordan (4:7, 22)
3. To provide an occasion to instruct children regarding the Red Sea
    crossing (v. 23)
4. To provide the occasion to exalt God among the nations (v. 24a)
5. To provide an occasion to generate the fear of the Lord in the hearts
    of his people for all generations (v. 24b)

The stones testified to a great fact, a great miracle, a great crossing,
and a great beginning of a new era in the lives of the Israelites. The land
memorial is set up at Gilgal. It is called *Gilgal* because the word means to
roll, like a stone, and is used figuratively (5:9) to speak of the shame of the
slavery and rebellion that God removed from Israel. God instructs Joshua to
circumcise all the men since this practice was abandoned in the wilderness
(5:5). The *Passover* was observed here for the first time since Mount Sinai
(Num. 9:1) two years after leaving Egypt. And the manna ceased as they
began to eat of the fruit of the land. There was much truth to be taught
when the children inquired as to the meaning of the pile of stones. Here
was a great and momentous mark of God's grace and the fulfillment of His
promises to the Israelites.

---

[25]   See discussion in Howard, David M. Jr. *The New American Commentary: Joshua*. See also, Bratcher,
Robert G. *A Handbook on the Book of Joshua*. Logos Bible Software

There is a real sense in which Israel, as a covenant people, were being born again. God was starting over with them as they entered the Promised Land. It was important that each generation should teach the next generation about the hand of God in their existence. The symbolism of the stone memorial was to be a major tool in teaching the next generation this reality.

American Christians have failed on both the civil and the religious front to utilize their respective symbols to teach the next generation. Family after family that I deal with in my counseling ministry has church roots with few, if any, fruits. When I walk these folks through the Bible to challenge their idolatry and identify their sin, they are frequently amazed that they have not been taught these things, even though they have been in the church. In the same manner, I talk with so many American Christians who are ignorant of the biblical foundations of this country, even though they are well-educated.

We have memorials in both the church and the state that we can utilize to teach our children about the hand of God. As teachers of the next generation, we can use the failure in the civil arena to illustrate what happens when we fail to capitalize on memorials for instruction. For example, we have failed to communicate very effectively the symbolism of putting the hand over the heart at the singing of the national anthem as a picture of our loyalty to our heritage. Observe at any sporting event the multitude of people who no longer practice this symbolism. It has become a pile of stones with no meaning. In the church the failure to teach both the corporate and personal meaning of the cross has produced a symbol that is all too often but *a pile of stones*. When we fail to teach the truth that memorials represent, they become piles of stones!

At my church, in Alabama, we have a pile of stones in one of the central locations on our property. Whenever you walk from one building to another, or when the children go outside to play, you can see the *ebenezer*. Parents can point to it and tell the children of God's faithfulness to our congregation. Those who are in their maturity can use it to teach younger couples. Our pastors have a continual reminder of God's unchanging grace. What are the memorials in your life? As a Christian Patriot, what action steps can you take this week to begin a life of commemoration with your family, your church, and your country?

Prayer:

O, God of Abraham, Isaac, and Jacob, grant us the wisdom to draw on these Old Testament memorials to provoke our children to ask what they mean! Help us to particularly utilize the New Testament sacraments as memorials to occasion the teaching of our children as to the hand of God in our lives. And, Lord, grant us also the wisdom to utilize the civil memorials to teach our children about the hand of God in the founding and preservation of our nation. Amen!

Action Steps:

ACTION STEP 1

Date Completed _____
Outcome

ACTION STEP 2

Date Completed _____
Outcome

ACTION STEP 3

Date Completed _____
Outcome

Week 43   Date: _____
A Pastor Calls Out Our National Sin
Text: *Deuteronomy 32:28–35*

Weekly Reading:
As often as we speak of a lack of true Christian Patriots and statesmen in our country and, particularly, in our legislature and politics, it is good to remember that there are those in ministry who have stepped forward and, for better or worse, attempted to bring conviction to the heart of our political system. This interesting prayer delivered at an opening session of the Kansas House of Representatives is an example of this.[26] After its delivery in Kansas, the prayer was subsequently read as an invocation in the Colorado House and broadcast by Paul Harvey. When Minister Joe Wright delivered this prayer, no doubt everyone was expecting the usual generalities, but here is what they heard:

> Heavenly Father, we come before you today to ask your forgiveness and to seek your direction and guidance. We know Your Word says, "Woe to those who call evil good," but that is exactly what we have done.
>
> We have lost our spiritual equilibrium and reversed our values.
> We have exploited the poor and call it the lottery.
> We have rewarded laziness and call it welfare.
> We have killed our unborn and called it choice.
> We have shot abortionists and call it justifiable.
> We have neglected to discipline our children and call it building self esteem.
> We have abused power and called it politics.
> We have coveted our neighbor's possessions and call it ambition.
> We have polluted the air with profanity and pornography and called it freedom of expression.
> We have ridiculed the time-honored values of our forefathers and call it enlightenment.
>
> Search us, O God, and know our hearts; cleanse us from every sin and set us free. Amen.

---

[26] Prayer may be found in numerous websites. Historical accuracy has been verified by TruthOrFiction.com accessed May 27, 2011.

It is well for Christian Patriots, in light of the charges leveled by Pastor Wright in his prayer, to give careful consideration to the first proposition of Jonathan Edwards's sermon, *Sinners in the Hands of an Angry God*. These words should bring us to repentance and revival lest as a nation we suffer the anger of God, who has so richly blessed us:

> There is no want of power in God to cast wicked men into hell at any moment. Men's hands cannot be strong when God rises up. The strongest have no power to resist him, nor can any deliver out of his hands. He is not only able to cast wicked men into hell, but he can most easily do it. Sometimes an earthly prince meets with a great deal of difficulty to subdue a rebel, who has found means to fortify himself, and has made himself strong by the numbers of his followers. But it is not so with God. There is no fortress that is any defense from the power of God. Though hand joins in hand, and vast multitudes of God's enemies combine and associate themselves, they are easily broken in pieces. They are as great heaps of light chaff before the whirlwind; or large quantities of dry stubble before devouring flames. We find it easy to tread on and crush a worm that we see crawling on the earth; so it is easy for us to cut or singe a slender thread that anything hangs by: thus easy is it for God, when he pleases, to cast his enemies down to hell. What are we that we should think to stand before him, at whose rebuke the earth trembles, and before whom the rocks are thrown down?[27]

Prayer:
Most Holy and Righteous God, we are appalled at our sin. You have granted us religious and political freedom. You have given us greater access to your Word than any nation on the face of the earth; yet, Father, we have neglected truth and replaced it with lies. We have called right wrong and wrong right and thereby justified our sin both nationally and personally. Grant us repentance and revival, lest you discipline us by those more wicked than we are. Shake and reshape our nation through vigorous and righteous preaching, even as you did in the founding of our nation.

---

[27]   Jonathan Edwards, *Sinners in the Hands of an Angry God*. Public Domain.

Action Steps:

ACTION STEP 1

Date Completed _____
Outcome

ACTION STEP 2

Date Completed _____
Outcome

ACTION STEP 3

Date Completed _____
Outcome

Week 44   Date: _____
Patterns of Education for the Christian Patriot
Text: *2 Timothy 2:1–2*

Weekly Reading:
At the beginning of our year together, I began my Preface by discussing my basic philosophy of Christian education. It is no coincidence that education as a general practice has appeared on numerous occasions throughout the course of these devotionals. Nor is it an aphorism to say that anywhere Christianity goes, education goes right along with it. Christians are people of the Book. Unfortunately for many within Christendom, the Book has become a symbol of religious heritage rather than the source of knowledge to understand God's purpose and the power to execute life in a godly manner. A great percentage of the universities in England, Europe, and America are rooted in the Christian tradition and were established not only to train men for the ministry but to prepare people for every walk of life with a liberal arts education that produced a Christian worldview.

The Christian life is learned. We do not have an experience-driven faith. We have a *knowing* faith. Our faith certainly has wonderful experiences, but they are appreciated by our knowledge of God. Here are five observations from 2 Timothy 2:1–2 that encapsulate this reality:[28]

1. The Christian life is transferred by intentional learning (content [doctrine], conformity [training], and cause [purpose for life]).
2. The Christian life is a matter of intentional learning ("thy word have I hid in my heart that I might not sin against you" Ps. 119:11).
3. The Christian life is learned; therefore, it is incumbent that we have faithful teachers who walk the talk and teach the content.
4. The Christian life is learned; therefore, we must choose teachers and mentors prayerfully (since teachers can only take you where they have been).
5. The Christian life is learned; therefore, every Christian must commit to teaching others (else it dies with you).

There are many patterns from the Judeo-Christian tradition that are instructive for the Christian with regard to his patriotic life. For example, the apostles were willing to obey religious and civil authorities so long as those

---

[28]   Refined from a sermon preached by Dr. Harry Reeder at Briarwood Presbyterian Church on May 15, 2011.

authorities did not circumscribe their preaching of the Gospel. Peter and John exemplified the principle in their answer to the authorities: "Whether it is right in the sight of God to give heed to you rather than to God, you judge; for we cannot stop speaking what we have seen and heard (Acts 4:19–20)." So, in this passage from Timothy we have five principles that apply to our patriotic life.

First, the American life is transferred by intentional learning. The history and the documents that emerged must be learned. The principles embodied are not intuitive. Training in the cultural nuances of a democratic republic must be rooted in these documents. The cause of "liberty and justice for all" must be framed by the Judeo-Christian heritage out of which it emanated. Second, since the American way is a matter of intentional learning, we must immerse our children, our families, our schools, and our immigrants in the founding documents and the historical context so that they might not be corrupted by the many attacks from the *wolves* (Acts 20:29–30) within and without. Third, we must have (and be) faithful teachers who walk the talk of historical Americanism and teach its content. Fourth, each of us must choose mentors and leaders who symbolize the best of America. Fifth, since the American Way is learned, each of us must take responsibility to become teachers of the American Way.

It is no coincidence that the people who have had the most lasting impact on the American way of life were either Christians, or they were men and women who had not lost the moral compass fostered by Christianity. If it is not to be us, Christian Patriots who lead, then it will be the men and women of society who are so driven by greed and ambition and personal gain. Those who lack principled conviction will not be able to stand up to them. As mentioned in an earlier reading, this is why Hitler came to power in Germany in the 1930s. But this should not happen in America. We who are Christians are best prepared to be Patriots. We are best prepared because of our Christian worldview and we are best prepared by the pattern of the Christian life. We have been given a touchstone of belief, a memorial of grace, a pattern of education, a foundation of morality and freedom to operate, and, most importantly, a Savior who does indeed save. But we must commit to passing this on to the coming generations. Will you, Christian Patriot, do so even this week?

Prayer:
We come to you, Father, with hearts filled with gratefulness and humility that you have granted us who are citizens of your Kingdom the privilege to be born and live in these United States. Grant us the courage and determination to transfer to our children, and the immigrants that join us, the knowledge to perpetuate the blessings of America. But first of all, grant that we would transfer the reality of the eternal Gospel to our children and our fellow citizens, without which the blessings of America are worthless commodities of time.

Action Steps:

ACTION STEP 1

Date Completed _____
Outcome

ACTION STEP 2

Date Completed _____
Outcome

ACTION STEP 3

Date Completed _____
Outcome

Week 45
Jesus to Congress
Text: *Matthew 23*

Date: _____

Weekly Reading:
Today's reading is one of the most fascinating pieces of biblical text I have had the opportunity to study in my Christian life. In this passage we have one of the most blistering indictments of leadership found in history. Jesus takes up the office of prophet—a speaker of truth—and sounds much like his Old Testament predecessors, only amped up on steroids! As a Christian Patriot, I have always wondered what this passage would sound like if Jesus were standing in our legislative halls today. Or, what would it sound like if Jesus were to address a joint session of Congress? A bit of poetic license would perhaps suggest something like the following. Imagine Jesus standing before our elected representatives, reading his own words as recorded in Scripture, and then commenting on them:

> **Verses 1–12**   Gentlemen, each of you desires to leave office remembered as a great leader. To achieve this you must first humble yourself and be a servant.

> **Verses 13–15**   Integrity is an essential quality of leadership. You must practice integrity in your religious life, integrity in your public policy, and integrity in your political philosophy.

> **Verses 16–22**   Transparency insulates you from demonstrable criticism and relieves you of the burden of defending what you say with elaborate schemes.

> **Verses 23–24**   Appropriate compassion exercised in justice and mercy is not only right in the sight of God, it ensures a clear conscience and rings true with the electorate.

> **Verses 25–26**   Honesty is essential for any leader, especially for one who holds a public trust. You cannot afford to look good on the outside in order to cover a corrupt heart. When your heart's desires are corrupt, be honest enough to admit them and "clean the inside of the cup."

Verses 27–36   Congruity or accuracy in the portrayal of history is critical. When you misrepresent history to advance your devious and misguided agendas, you distort the hand of Providence.[29]

He of course would illustrate each of these points with appropriate current events, of which there are, sadly, plenty of transgressions from which to choose. I believe sincerely that in today's environment there would be a scattered applause at best and no standing ovation.

As Christian Patriots our hearts are deeply saddened by this scene. However, it is important to remember that we, by our failure to engage the public arena, have contributed to the current situation. Over the past sixty years the evangelical community has largely withdrawn from the political scene. We have not populated the county commissions, the school boards, the city councils, and the like. Too often we have left the body politic to the world while we tended to the church or our own private little community. We have fallen into the world's trap of separation of church and state. Unfortunately, this kind of separation is neither biblical nor productive.

So what are Christian Patriots to do? First, we must insist on political leaders living by these six character traits. Second, we must become participants in the system. We must educate, prepare, and encourage one another to engage this messy business of running a nation. Third, we must find ways to cast the vision to our children to re-create an America that is what America was founded to be. Fourth, and most importantly, we must preach the Gospel that transforms lives and we must disciple these lives with a biblical worldview, which, in turn, will produce people who both want to and are able to lead our nation in the pattern of our forefathers.

Prayer:
Dear Jesus, address Congress through your people. Grant us such an impact that the nation is transformed by the Gospel. Lord, our only hope is the Gospel. Grant us an army of young men and women who are captured by what you did in and through our forefathers so that they will generate a revival of justice and righteousness in the church and in the land. Grant us to remember, to repent, and to revive what we have known. Amen.

---

[29]   Please understand that it is not my intent to pervert the Scriptures. I am taking poetic license in order to make a practical application to our political leaders of the principles embedded in Jesus' message to the religious leaders.

Action Steps:

ACTION STEP 1

Date Completed _____
Outcome

ACTION STEP 2

Date Completed _____
Outcome

ACTION STEP 3

Date Completed _____
Outcome

Week 46   Date: _____
George Washington
on Divine Providence and Divine Dependence
Text: *Psalm 57*

Weekly Reading:
We often forget that many of the Psalms were written by a king, and often in the midst of volatile and highly charged political situations. David wrote this psalm when he was being hotly pursued by Saul. He believed that his cause was righteous and that God would be his defender. Yet he was aware of his precarious situation and sought God's intervention while declaring his confidence that "I will give thanks to Thee, O Lord, among the peoples; I will sing praises to thee among the nations." We see parallels in our early Founding Fathers, who turned to the Lord in the midst of difficult and harrowing times.

After a lengthy statement assessing his own inadequacies, President Washington, in his inaugural address as president, launched into an acknowledgement of Divine Providence in the establishment of America. He leaves no doubt that he believes it self-evident that the Almighty Being has guided every step by "some token of providential agency."

> *Such being the impressions under which I have, in obedience to the public summons, repaired to the present station, it would be peculiarly improper to omit in this first official act my fervent supplications to that Almighty Being who rules over the universe, who presides in the councils of nations, and whose providential aids can supply every human defect, that His benediction may consecrate to the liberties and happiness of the people of the United States a Government instituted by themselves for these essential purposes, and may enable every instrument employed in its administration to execute with success the functions allotted to his charge. In tendering this homage to the Great Author of every public and private good, I assure myself that it expresses your sentiments not less than my own, nor those of my fellow-citizens at large less than either. No people can be bound to acknowledge and adore the Invisible Hand which conducts the affairs of men more than those of the United States. Every step by which they have advanced to the character of an independent nation seems to have been distinguished*

by some token of providential agency; and in the important revolution just accomplished in the system of their united government the tranquil deliberations and voluntary consent of so many distinct communities from which the event has resulted cannot be compared with the means by which most governments have been established without some return of pious gratitude, along with an humble anticipation of the future blessings which the past seem to presage. These reflections, arising out of the present crisis, have forced themselves too strongly on my mind to be suppressed. You will join with me, I trust, in thinking that there are none under the influence of which the proceedings of a new and free government can more auspiciously commence.

Washington follows this affirmation of the work of Divine Providence with a statement that outlines his anticipated relationship with Congress and a personal policy regarding compensation. He then closes his inaugural address with the following declaration of the American people's dependence on the "Parent of the Human Race" on which "the success of this Government must depend:"

Having thus imparted to you my sentiments as they have been awakened by the occasion which brings us together, I shall take my present leave; but not without resorting once more to the benign Parent of the Human Race in humble supplication that, since He has been pleased to favor the American people with opportunities for deliberating in perfect tranquility, and dispositions for deciding with unparalleled unanimity on a form of government for the security of their union and the advancement of their happiness, so His divine blessing may be equally conspicuous in the enlarged views, the temperate consultations, and the wise measures on which the success of this Government must depend.[30]

Fellow Christian Patriot, here is our threefold challenge. First, we must determine to emulate the values and leadership of Washington. Will we acknowledge Divine Providence in the establishment of this nation and determine to be consciously dependent on the Divine in the execution of

---

[30]   Washington's inaugural address is public domain and can be found at numerous websites, particularly in the National Archives.

self-governing? Second, we must determine to raise and educate a coming generation who will take up the challenge of reviving Washington's form of patriotism. Third, we must pray for the Lord to raise a group of uniquely gifted leaders like unto our Founding Fathers who can recalibrate our national soul, and, more than that, we must be willing to become those leaders ourselves.

Prayer:

Father, from whom comes every good gift, grant us leaders who will humble themselves before you and who will have the capacity to lead us in self-governing that seeks the benefit of all peoples. Lord, you made us a great nation to provide a great opportunity for the Gospel. Would you restore that greatness and protect that opportunity. And, Lord, would you help me to be willing to be your instrument to achieve this good. Amen.

Action Steps:

ACTION STEP 1

Date Completed _____
Outcome

ACTION STEP 2

Date Completed _____
Outcome

ACTION STEP 3

Date Completed _____
Outcome

Week 47   Date: _____

The Bible and the Tone for Colonial American Leadership

Text: *I Timothy 3:1–16*

Weekly Reading:

If you desire an interesting exercise in American history, go to this website, www.ushistory.org, and read the thumbnail biographical sketches of the signers of the Declaration of Independence.[31] It is a fascinating read in which the accounts yield two consistent and almost universal facts about these men. First, they were characterized by faith in the God of the Bible and the practice of a morality that flowed from the Judeo-Christian framework.[32] Second, they had a love of country demonstrated in lifelong service to the public welfare, often at personal expense. They were flawed human beings (men with feet of clay) but they possessed what we might call a consensus of desirable traits.

As a whole, they were men of character who could be depended on. Take, for example, James Wilson, who found himself in a bind. Pennsylvania was divided on the issue of separation from England, and Wilson had written eloquently in favor of independence. He refused to vote, however, against the will of his constituents who it appeared did not favor independence. He returned home for three weeks to consult with those he represented. When the vote came he was able to affirm that Pennsylvania was in favor of independence, because he worked together with them.

They were men of breadth. They were well-educated and well-read, often teaching themselves. They represented diverse professions that ranged from farmer, to lawyer, to merchant, to banker, to physician, to university professor.

They were creative and innovative. They crafted the unique instruments of government that became the basis of our nation. They developed an import/export business that not only rivaled but surpassed that of their British homeland.

They were men of common sense, who understood that government was necessary to provide a secure context in which free people could prosper.

---

[31] http://www.ushistory.org/declaration/signers/index.htm

[32] http://www.adherents.com/gov/Founding_Fathers_Religion.html This site lists 204 Founding Fathers. Of these 204, 167 were affiliated with some Christian denomination. Eighty-eight were Episcopalian and thirty were Presbyterian.

They also understood that less was more when it comes to government. A free people must take responsibility for the exercise of freedom if they are to retain their freedom.

They were men of tenacity. They crafted a vision that became their goal. They made the commitment to obtain that goal. They were resolute in their pursuit of the goal. For many it cost them their lives and/or their fortunes.

Benjamin Harrison is a good example of these traits. Harrison was an Episcopalian from Virginia. He attended William and Mary College in Williamsburg. Unfortunately, as the result of the tragic death of his father and two sisters in a lightning storm, he was not able to graduate. At age 38 he was elected to the House of Burgesses. In 1764, when the House defied the Royal Governor and passed the Stamp Act Resolutions, the Governor offered Harrison an appointment to the executive council if he were to remain a loyalist. He refused the appointment. Instead, he launched a devoted campaign for republican principles. He was elected to the Continental Congress in 1774, and the following year joined General Washington in Cambridge to plan the future of the American Army. He served as a lieutenant in his county militia. Subsequently, he was chosen Speaker of the House in 1778, and completed his public service by being elected governor of the State of Virginia in 1782. He was disciplined, a man of principle and conviction, and a man who developed his many talents. These men were Christian Patriots.

Overall, the biblical model for leadership qualifications set the tone for the qualifications of Colonial leadership. These qualifications were not so much prescribed as they were assumed as a result of the prescriptions for leadership in the church. In other words, because the church was so prominent in society, as thinking and active members, the paradigm of biblical leadership was already established in our government. Ask yourself, Christian Patriot, who is establishing the model of leadership today?

Prayer:
Father in heaven, we would pray that your will be done on earth as it is in heaven. Grant us leaders, grant us to be leaders, who meet your qualifications for service in your church and then we shall once again have national leaders of character. Forgive us wherein we have failed to choose such leaders. Grant us repentance and revival. Amen.

Action Steps:

ACTION STEP 1

Date Completed _____
Outcome

ACTION STEP 2

Date Completed _____
Outcome

ACTION STEP 3

Date Completed _____
Outcome

Week 48   Date: _____
A Christian Patriot Prays for Personal Revival
Text: *Psalm 119:33–40*

Weekly Reading:
We are nearing the end of our year-long journey together. We have contemplated and examined the need for thinking, passionate, and action-oriented Christian Patriots. We have prayed model patriotic prayers together. I trust we leave this time together prepared for a lifetime of patriotic action, motivated and fueled by the centrality of our faith. The entire Bible—as well as every Christian's experience—is witness to our need for regular, constant, and intentional revival. In this passage the psalmist provides us with a great model for how the Christian Patriot should pray for personal revival.

His prayer begins with the expression of his heart of commitment (Ps. 119:33). If you will teach me your statutes, Lord, I will observe them. What does this commitment look like for the Christian Patriot? First, it means I will love the Lord my God with all my heart, all my strength, and all my soul. It means that I will honor God in the manner in which I conduct the business of life. It means that I will do all that I do with the intention of glorifying God. Therefore, it secondarily means that as an American Patriot I will be committed to my responsibility to intentionally uphold the Constitution and to work to see that the laws of the land remain consistent with the Constitution.

The psalmist then articulates a plea for enablement (vv.34–35). He is well aware from his own experience and the experience of his nation that he cannot keep this commitment without the enabling power of God. His plea consists of two verbs. The first verb is "give." The psalmist realizes that in order for him to properly observe God's law, God must give him understanding. O, how the Christian Patriot needs a God-given understanding of God's Word in order to know how to observe it in his civil life! The second verb is "make." The Hebrew word is a straightforward translation into English. It simply means "to compel." Compel me, O God, to walk in the path of your commandments so that I might keep my commitments. He gives two reasons for his prayer beyond keeping his commitment to observe God's Word to the end (v. 33). His two reasons are these. He wants to keep God's law with all his heart (v. 34), and he delights in God's Word (v. 35).

But living out this commitment is a task beyond his personal capacity. Thus, the psalmist admits his weakness (vv. 36–37). In verse 36 his request is a contrast. Grant to me [incline] a bent toward the path of life that your commands dictate and don't let me be caught up with my natural bent toward wealth.[33] Verse 37 is a similar contrast: turn away my eyes from worthless things and rather refocus me toward your values. In a nation where we have so much opportunity to have, accumulate, and pursue wealth—material things—it is easy for us to lose sight of our commitments to God and our responsibilities as patriots. We need to pray "Revive me in your ways!" (v. 37)

The psalmist closes with three specific pleas (vv. 38–40). First, let your Word, O God, produce reverence for you (38). Second, help me live in a manner that will protect me from the deserved reproach of violating your ordinances (39). Third, grant that the observation of your righteousness through your precepts will revive me. These may be summed up in the following way: restore the vigor of life by your righteousness whenever I need it in order that I might reverence [literally, fear] you.

In this Psalm we see the beautiful and yet inexplicable interrelationship of grace and responsibility. As Christian Patriots we are completely dependent on grace to exercise responsibility, yet we are responsible.

Prayer:
O, Father, hear my prayer! I desire to observe your Word in my manner of life. But, Father, I am weak and given to seeing and experiencing this life through my flesh. I am prone to seek wealth for my pleasure. I am prone to be self-absorbed and therefore not exercise mercy and justice. I need you, Lord, to give me understanding, to make me walk uprightly, to incline my heart to your Word, to turn my eyes from vanity and revive me in your righteousness. Do this, Lord, that I might be the Christian you have called me to be and a citizen that represents you well. Grant me a life of grace that I might glorify you in all of life.

---

[33] The word inclined means disposed. The word *dishonest* gain does not necessarily mean *dishonest*, but rather great wealth.

Action Steps:

ACTION STEP 1

Date Completed _____
Outcome

ACTION STEP 2

Date Completed _____
Outcome

ACTION STEP 3

Date Completed _____
Outcome

Week 49   Date: _____
Transforming Culture:
One Citizen, One City, One Country at a Time
Text: *Titus 1–3*

Weekly Reading:
Crete was multicultural and multireligious. These conditions characterized the island for centuries. It is into this culture that the apostle Paul sent his disciple, Titus, to organize the Cretan church. The result was the development of a strong church as is evidenced by the influence observed from Crete for the next 900 years.

America was once such a culture rooted in the Judeo-Christian ethic. The culture of contemporary America, however, is rapidly devolving into a pagan society which can be observed in art, music, philosophy, religion, and even in the public demeanor. The Philadelphia "thuggings" (a term coined by the Philadelphia press) of 2011 are an example. What is at the root of this evil behavior? Paul warns what will happen, "When he who restrains is taken out of the way" (2 Thess. 2:7). Think of the history of Africa in the 1800s when missionaries arrived. Or read the biography of John Paton regarding the conditions of the peoples of the New Hebrides when he arrived in the nineteenth century. Yet in 2010, a colleague who was teaching at a seminary in the Philippines had only two students from these islands. He asked about the percentage of Christians there today. They answered, "About 95 percent." He asked how many of the Christians were Presbyterian (John Paton was a Presbyterian). They answered, "About 95 percent!" You see, when the Gospel moves in and people are converted, the Holy Spirit becomes present, restraint is established, and culture is transformed.

England and America are not far behind—in *banishing* the Holy Spirit. Gospel conversions have declined. Church attendance, where the Holy Spirit influences believers through worship and preaching, has declined. The Word of God is struck more and more from the public square. Hence, He who restrains is taken out of the way. What you have left is the unrestrained human heart, the character of which Jeremiah reminds us in 17:9 is "more deceitful than all else and is desperately wicked; who can understand it?" What you saw in the London riots of the summer of 2011 and the "thuggings" on the streets of Philadelphia is the action of unrestrained evil hearts.

Paul planted a church in such a society in Crete—he took a beachhead. He now sends in *General Titus* to develop an occupational force. There are three challenges set before him.

The first challenge is the establishment of leadership in the church (Titus, ch. 1). This is the main thrust of the first part of the book of Titus. Colonial America probably had more qualified and gifted leaders per square inch than any nation in history. There was a great deal of tension, but biblical character forestalled its outbreak. Today we are lacking this character—just look at how many politicians cannot keep their sexual behavior above reproach.

The second challenge Titus received regarded the leadership of the local church and the church at large. Christians are to live contrasting lifestyles (ch. 2). The populace should be able to distinguish Christians from non-Christians by observing their behavior. Older men, older women, younger women, and younger men are "in all things [to] show [themselves] to be an example of good deeds, with purity in doctrine, dignified, sound in speech which is above reproach" (vv. 7–8).

The third challenge is to live out the Christian life in the public square (ch. 3). Christians are to be subject to authorities, engaged in good deeds, shunning foolish controversies, and rejecting those who are factious. In other words, Christians should speak out in the public square after having gained credibility by engaging in good deeds that meet pressing needs so that our lives are not unfruitful (v. 14). The substance of what we say is backed by lives that concretely practice the doctrine we proclaim.

Prayer:
Holy Father, enable me to pursue holiness so that my Christian Patriot cry for a return to our roots rings true in the public square! Grant me wisdom to determine pressing needs, the willingness to sacrifice to minister to those needs, and both the passion and the words to speak powerfully in the public square. Help me, Father, not to be intimidated by the factious man and to recognize foolish controversies so that I might avoid them. Grant me to be a person of influence wherever you place me for the sake of the Kingdom of God and the transforming of the culture of my country and thereby the world. Amen.

Action Steps:

ACTION STEP 1

Date Completed _____
Outcome

ACTION STEP 2

Date Completed _____
Outcome

ACTION STEP 3

Date Completed _____
Outcome

Week 50   Date: _____
Nehemiah: An Example of a Nation Rebuilder
Text: *Nehemiah 1:1–2:4*

Weekly Reading:
The walls of Jerusalem were broken down and the gates were burned after the Babylonians raided the city in 586 BC. Israel, both north and south, had rebelled against God. Again and again He sent prophets to rebuke and warn them of impending judgment if they continued on this trajectory. Artaxerxes was the third king of Persia that God used to effect a movement of restoration that started with Ezra and the temple rebuilding under Zerubbabel. He empowered Nehemiah to return and rebuild the walls of Jerusalem.

Like Nehemiah, we are faced with a country whose walls have been torn down. The walls of our country, erected on the foundation of Judeo-Christian ethics and beliefs, are being systematically destroyed. The barbarians are attacking at the gates. Like Nehemiah, we have access to those in power. And, like Nehemiah, we must rise to the challenge.

Nehemiah, like Daniel, ascended to an important role in the pagan kingdom. The king's cupbearer would be similar to being director of the Secret Service in a US administration. He was admired and valued by the king and charged with the king's safety. Nevertheless, although he had a position of great prominence in a pagan kingdom, Nehemiah had a great concern for his own nation, and no doubt regularly sought information from travelers regarding conditions there. Such is the case recorded here as he inquired of Hanani, one of his brothers, of the condition of the city of Jerusalem (1:2). The description of Jerusalem was twofold: the people were in distress and the walls were in ruin.

Nehemiah's response is instructive for us today. As we have seen over and over throughout this year, the response of those in ancient Israel can help us in our response to our country today. So what did Nehemiah do? He prayed. His prayer consisted of seven elements:

1.   Emotional expression of his pain over the condition of his nation—"I wept and mourned for days" (Nehemiah 1:4)
2.   Intense engagement with God—"I was fasting and praying before the God of heaven" (v. 4)

3. Adoration of God (v. 5)
4. Confession of his and the nation's sin (v. 6–7)
5. Pleading the promises of God (v. 8–11a)
6. Personal request for successful fulfillment of daily responsibilities (v. 11b)
7. Request for providential arrangements (v. 11c)

Following his prayer (which should be understood as ongoing), Nehemiah lived with the anticipation of a God-made opportunity to take action. This came four months later, after he had been given the news by Hanani. Nehemiah is serving the king when the king asks, "What would you request?" Nehemiah reports that he prayed to the God of heaven (Ok, Lord, this is it. I am depending on you!). "And I said to the King . . . ." God granted the king "compassion before this man" (v. 11c), who authorized and equipped Nehemiah to rebuild the walls of Jerusalem. While he achieved this project with incredible rapidity, it was not without opposition, even though he had the authority of the king to empower him.

We have not been overrun by another nation, but we have been overrun by a pagan philosophy that touches every dimension of our national life. The walls have been broken down—biblical doctrine has been diluted and the church has become anemic. The gates have been burned in institution after institution, both academically and socially. They lie in ruin. The remnants who have survived the captivity of this pagan takeover are in distress.

We are in need of a cadre of men like Nehemiah. A call to Christian Patriotism is a call to the prayer of Nehemiah. Will you humble yourself before the Lord with emotional fasting and prayer for the church and America? Will you express your adoration to the God of our forefathers for who He is and for His gracious gift of spiritual freedom through the work of Christ on the cross and the political gift of freedom in the Constitution and Bill of Rights? Will you join hands with other believers in expressing repentance for our sin—we have neglected to guard what has been entrusted to our care (I Tim. 6:20; 2 Tim. 1:14) by our forefathers of the faith and of the nation. Will you plead the promises of God (2 Chron. 7:14) for restoration? Will you pray for success in living your own godly life and serve enthusiastically in the church and in the nation? Will you pray for providential arrangements (Col. 4:3) and will you live anticipating the opportunity to act?

Nehemiah lived intentionally! We are called to live intentionally by making disciples. We are called to live intentionally by living out our faith in every arena of life, including that of citizenship. In America that means taking responsibility for self-governing. As we approach the end of our study, think of all we have learned this year. How can you, like Nehemiah, rebuild the walls of our nation for the glory of God? Praise His name! We can be his instruments to rebuild the walls.

Prayer:
O, gracious Father, we adore you. You are not only the creator of all things, but you are the giver of every good and perfect gift. We thank you for the gift of the American republic rooted and grounded in your Word. We confess, Lord, we have failed to guard your Word, which in turn has led to the broken-down walls and burned gates in the church and the nation. Father, we repent and ask that you give us the grace to live in repentance and dependence. We ask for success in daily living so that we might live with anticipation of the opportunities to rebuild the walls and the gates. Grant us the tenacity to hold a trowel in one hand and your Sword in the other so that we might build and defend the gifts that you have given. Amen.

Action Steps:

ACTION STEP 1

Date Completed _____
Outcome

ACTION STEP 2

Date Completed _____
Outcome

ACTION STEP 3

Date Completed _____
Outcome

Week 51   Date: _____
Our Model of Citizenship
Text: *I Timothy 4:11–16*

Weekly Reading:
We are coming to the end of our year. How do we move on to the next level? How do we make this our way of life, and not just a small part of life? What are the last things I could say to you? It's simple. The Christian Patriot must keep his patriotism in biblical perspective. The Kingdom of God must always take precedence (Phil. 1:15–23; Heb. 1:2). It is the Gospel that saves a sinner, not political freedom or the American democratic republic. It is the love of Christ that enlivens the church (Rev. 2:1–8). It is the Gospel-driven Christian who inspires the moral compass of the nation, as detailed in the Constitution and Bill of Rights (Matt. 5:14).

Paul articulates six important principles for church leaders for the health of the church that are transferable to Patriots for the health of the nation. They are found in I Timothy 4:11–16.

1. Practice being an unabashed example of character (4:12)
2. Practice perpetual reading of the primary documents (4:14)
3. Practice perpetual exhortation to commitment (4:14)
4. Practice perpetual teaching of the basics (4:14)
5. Practice personal immersion in the basics (4:15)
6. Practice persistent personal surveillance (4:16)

In chapter five, verse 20, Paul summarizes this thinking again when he writes, "O Timothy, guard the deposit entrusted to you [intentional vigilance]. Avoid the irreverent babble and contradictions of what is falsely called knowledge [anything inconsistent with the biblical worldview], for by professing it some have swerved from the faith. *Grace be with you.*"

Paul and other apostles were the consummate models of citizenship. Their focus was on the work of the ministry and the establishment of the kingdom through church planting and church revitalization within the jurisdiction of Rome and beyond. Therefore, observing the apostles' lives gives us a clear picture of a Christian manner of life within a political system. Obviously we do not see them engaged in the kind of political activities characteristic of a democratic republic. However, a close scrutiny of their teaching and actions is instructive for us in our context. Here are seven observations for our consideration.

1. We note that the apostles recognized that the Roman government and its appointees were under God's direction (Rom. 13:1).
2. They taught that to disobey the government was to disobey God (Rom. 13:2).
3. The apostles observed that God established government for the well-being of society (Rom. 13:3).
4. They illustrated proper use of government for personal safety in the cause of the Gospel ("I appeal to Caesar" [Acts 16:35–40, 25:11]).
5. They demonstrated how to use nonviolent resistance (Acts 5:29–32).
6. The apostles used their citizenship to bear public witness and to establish self-defense (Acts 16:28–34; 21:37–40).
7. They practiced dignity in the public square even under duress (Acts 24:1–16)

The strength of the nation is in the strength of the church, and the strength of the church is in the strength of the believers. The strength of believers emanates from being Spirit-filled, living in obedience (Eph. 5:18); from being Christ-centered (Heb 12:1–2); and from being Gospel driven ("For I could wish that I myself were accursed and cut off from Christ for the sake of my brothers" Rom. 9:3). Creating and maintaining such an army of believers begins with you and me. An America populated with such believers who take up the responsibility of impacting their nation with the Christian worldview will be a free America.[34]

Prayer:
Almighty and everlasting God, grant us the ability to remember from whence we have departed, the desire to repent, and the determination to revive what we have been both as the church and as a nation. Yet, Father, we would desire above all that your will be done on earth, even as it is in heaven. We desire the return of Jesus and the restoration of all things. Yea, Lord, we desire the "more than redemption" that you have promised. We desire you! Amen!

---

[34] There is an aggressive opposition to our point of view. See http://www.ffrf.org/. This is the web site of Freedom from Religion Foundation. In the name of *free thought* the stated purpose of this organization has several objectives: promote separation of church and state, atheism, agnosticism and non-theism.

Action Steps:

ACTION STEP 1

Date Completed _____
Outcome

ACTION STEP 2

Date Completed _____
Outcome

ACTION STEP 3

Date Completed _____
Outcome

Week 52   Date: _____
Text: *Deuteronomy 4:9, 11:19; Psalm 22:31, 71:18, 102:18*

America
Megan Hendrick[35]

Feet in the sand
Hangin'n over the Grand Canyon
Moments of laughter with pure joy
Moments of moms losing their boys
They fight for the freedom's rights
for liberty we stand to fight.
Freedom to have God or not,
bring your culture to this spot.
A place where neighbors become brothers
Yes, it's not perfect, I know,
Trust me, our failure shows.
But through God's grace and mercy,
We'll make it back to the Almighty.
God built America for a purpose,
so take heart Fellow American!
Though we do wrong, horrific things,
the Heart of America will sing.
Holy, Holy is the Lord God Almighty
Who was, who is, and who is to come.
We give our God the glory
till Jesus comes to take us where He is from
So stand tall Christian American,
and begin your journey searching for the end.
Because we are America

Megan is my granddaughter who recently turned thirteen (2011). She is an athlete, a musician, a writer, and a straight-A student. I commissioned her to write a poetic piece to honor America. I have made only a few very minor edits to this work. Everything else is the work of an amazing thirteen-year-old girl who loves the Lord and her country. I trust it will be an encouragement to you. She is one of many young people who love God and country. Unfortunately, they are seldom recognized and are slighted

---

[35]   © Megan Hendrick 2011 and used by permission.

by media coverage. Pray for Megan and others like her. The future of this nation is in their hands, but their future is in the hands of the current ruling generation. We must take up the responsibility to hand off to coming generations both the legacy of freedom rooted in the structure that our forefathers gave to us, and a sustainable, debt-free economy. Megan and her generation will either begin a twenty-first-century enlightenment or they will suffer persecution for their stand for God and country. The American drift away from the Judeo-Christian moral framework inclines one to believe that it will, in all probability, be persecution. But that is not set in stone. And it is up to men and women like you and me to exercise our God-given responsibility to change that for Christ and country.

It is my hope that this year-long exercise in developing your philosophy of Christian Patriotism will motivate and enable you to contribute to refashioning America after her roots. The freedom to preach the Gospel is at stake. The freedom to oppose immorality is at stake. The freedom to conduct political debate is at stake. Thomas Jefferson in his first inaugural address said this:

> *These principles form the bright constellation which has gone before us and guided our steps through an age of revolution and reformation. The wisdom of our sages and blood of our heroes have been devoted to their attainment. They should be the creed of our political faith, the text of civil instruction, the touchstone by which to try the services of those we trust; and should we wander from them in moments of error or of alarm, let us hasten to retrace our steps and to regain the road which alone leads to peace, liberty, and safety.*[36]

The principles that empowered the *Great American Experiment* are these:
1. Recognition that individual rights are derived from a Creator.
2. Recognition that both general revelation (laws of nature) and special revelation (the nature of God) as revealed in Scripture are foundational.
3. Recognition of human imperfection and the tendency to abuse power.
4. Recognition of the need for a *king* to restrain threat of abuse.

---

[36] Visited August 4, 2011, http://www.nccs.net/articles/ril71.html.

5. Recognition of the need to utilize a written constitution to serve as *king* by carefully dividing, balancing, and separating the powers to provide a system of checks and balances on human power.

6. Recognition that all powers must be in the body politic (the people), who by consent delegate certain powers to government with the proviso of the disenfranchisement of those delegated powers if abused.

Christian, become a Christian Patriot. I can say it no more clearly than that. Be committed to aggressive evangelism. Be committed to personal holiness. Be committed to a humble recognition that your American heritage is a gift from God to be honored and protected as an instrument for the expansion of the Kingdom of God, and in the process to be a demonstration of the blessing of 2 Chronicles 7:14.[37]

So, before we close, let me ask you one last time: are you a Christian Patriot? In the Preface to this book I told you that I would give you the opportunity to outline your philosophy of Christian Patriotism. You have the Founding Fathers; you have memorials; you have the transference of blessings; you have a pattern of education; and, most importantly, you have Jesus Christ, who has saved you from your sins. What will your philosophy of Christian Patriotism be? Let me challenge you one last time: sit down with your husband or your wife, sit down with your children and tell them of your intention. What do you believe now and how will it affect your life and ministry, both individually and as a family? It's not truly a passion unless it comes out of your life and pours into others.

Prayer:
Allow me to finish our time together with one more prayer.

Father in heaven, we have come to the end of this year of intentional focus on you and your involvement in the providential establishment of America. We have, though imperfectly, engaged in developing our responsibility to be your instrument in preserving the gift of political and religious freedom. Lord, we would pray for the Megans of the next generation. May they be tenacious in their walk with you and in their engagement in being Christian Patriots! Enable them to faithfully articulate the Gospel so that they live out their dual citizenship unfailingly. Amen

---

[37] If my people, who are called by my name, will humble themselves and pray and seek my face and turn from their wicked ways, then I will hear from heaven, and I will forgive their sin and will heal their land. (NIV)

Action Steps:

ACTION STEP 1

Date Completed _____
Outcome

ACTION STEP 2

Date Completed _____
Outcome

ACTION STEP 3

Date Completed _____
Outcome

Epilogue

As I wrote this book, it became clear that while I have been very passionate about America, my practice of Christian Patriotism has been minimal. My profession has provided a platform to challenge and coach people in the development of their Christian life so that they could become capable of being salt and light. Being salt and light is the foundation on which the Constitution and Bill of Rights were built and gave rise to the American culture. My engagement in this project has led me to a commitment of practical engagement as a Christian Patriot that parallels my work in the spiritual development of people. In spite of our cultural condition, I am excited with anticipation at the prospect of revival. We have seen grass-roots movements make a difference. The women's suffrage movement enfranchised women as full-fledged members of our self-governing society. The civil rights movement generated the momentum to enfranchise African Americans. For nearly forty years since Roe v. Wade, grass-roots efforts have been gaining ground in the struggle to enfranchise unborn children. Grass-roots Christian Patriots can revive and protect our Constitution and the Bill of Rights and thereby our religious freedom to preach the Gospel at home and abroad.

We need this grass-roots movement to return our nation to its Judeo-Christian foundation. But such a movement will not start without commitment. Let me challenge you to join me in contributing to this movement. It is my prayer that at least 100,000 Americans will purchase this book and carry out its challenge. If that occurs and each reader does three projects a week, it will mean that 15,600,000 patriotic actions will be performed over the next year. But, if those original 100,000 will each give out five copies of this book and those recipients take up the challenge, there will be 4,680,000,000,000 Christian Patriotic actions accomplished. While the prospects of every reader engaging in three projects every week is a hope beyond reality, I am hopeful that such a grass-roots movement will become a groundswell of Christian Patriots, committed servants and voters who generate revival and reform.

With such a movement spawned by Charles Wesley and a handful of other leaders, God revived two continents and through them great portions of the world. I am praying that He will graciously do it again. Join me, please!

Howard A. Eyrich
James Hill Community
Hoover, AL

Appendix I

Possible Action Plans

While on a family vacation, my children and grandchildren (total of 15) sat around a dinner table and brainstormed to create this list of possible Action Plans for the Christian Patriot. This certainly is not an exhaustive list. It is a suggestive list to stimulate your thinking. Nonetheless, these suggestions can become your Action Plans as you begin this commitment. They will give you time and stimulus to create your own list. Perhaps you could engage your family in coming up with your own list and use the exercise to "fire up the troops" to join you in this journey.

1. Pray for your US senator or representative this week.
2. Take your mayor to lunch.
3. Pray for your state representatives this week.
4. Write a letter to a government representative.
5. Observe a jury trial this week.
6. Attend a local fund raiser for the party of your choice.
7. Register to vote if you have not already done so.
8. Research a candidate this week.
9. Read a biography of a Founding Father.
10. Plan to take your family to Colonial Williamsburg for vacation.
11. Plan to take your family this weekend to a local American historical site.
12. Make a donation to an American historical site preservation fund.
13. Read the Declaration of Independence this week, or have your family read it and discuss it.
14. Assign your children age-appropriate reading about early America and have a family night talking about the meaning and values they encountered.
15. Study flag etiquette with your family.
16. Choose one family meal a week at which you recite the Pledge of Allegiance together.
17. Visit or plan a visit to Washington, DC.
18. Do something patriotic with the family this week.
19. Visit a National Cemetery.
20. Send a care package to a member of the military.
21. Plan to educate your family on Patriotic Days (Memorial Day, Fourth of July).

22. Purchase and fly an American flag at your home.
23. Learn the thirteen colonies and the fifty states.
24. Visit your state capital.
25. Volunteer to serve at voting polls.
26. Interview a veteran.
27. Take a soldier to lunch and thank him/her for serving.
28. Read the Constitution.
29. Take an underprivileged child or teenager to a patriotic activity and treat him/her to the day.
30. Pray for active military personnel.
31. As a family read a historical document at each family meal this week.
32. Visit or plan a visit to a WW II memorial.
33. Watch *The Patriot* movie and discuss it.
34. Send a thank-you note to a local public servant (county commissioner, sheriff, etc.).
35. Look for a man (men) or woman (women) at lunch time and buy his/her lunch and express appreciation for service.
36. Read George Washington's Inaugural Address.
37. Watch a historically accurate military movie.
38. Investigate how to participate in local government.
39. Commit to pledging four (or two, or ten) hours a week to help a local candidate get elected.
40. Volunteer to assist a social studies teacher by preparing a special class on some aspect of Colonial America.
41. Commit to following an election and explaining to your children the importance of public service and the process of participating, through a weekly family discussion.
42. Encourage your local school to conduct mock elections at the state and national levels.
43. Assemble a collection of American Patriotic hymns and song and the story behind them and then lead your family once a week in a patriotic family night that incorporates the collection you assemble.
44. Volunteer to help students register to vote.
45. Volunteer to provide transportation to the polls for those needing transportation.
46. Volunteer to pass out literature during a campaign.
47. Arrange a prayer calendar through which you pray for every elected public servant of the next year who directly impacts your personal life.

48. Build community around an active military family.
49. Encourage your church to build community around the military families in your church (get a couple of families together over dinner and discuss how this can be done).
50. One of my family members suggested: Just find a need and commit to fill it.
51. Read a biography of a patriot to your grandchild this week.
52. Determine three people to whom you will give a copy of Washington's Inaugural Address this week.
53. Set up a rotation prayer list of your senators and congressmen/women and send them an email of your schedule.
54. Read a book this week on Colonial America.
55. Write an op-ed article for your local newspaper or community paper this week regarding a call to a Christian Patriot.
56. Take your son or daughter and some of their friends to visit an American memorial, then take them on a fun activity and finally to McDonald's, and over hamburgers ask them what they learned at the memorial about America and their responsibility as a citizen.
57. Memorize all the stanzas of the Star-Spangled Banner.
58. Interview a candidate for a local political office to determine his/her commitment to the American heritage.
59. Take a course on early American history and be prepared to commend or challenge the professor in terms of our true American heritage.
60. Purchase and display an American flag.
61. Start a conversation with a neighbor about the Founding Fathers.
62. If you are a student, write a paper about the providence of God in American history.
63. Use one of the essays in this devotional book to create a Sunday School lesson to teach on a national holiday weekend to a youth or children's class.
64. Invite several neighborhood families for a cookout and give each man a copy of this book. Encourage him to share it with his family.
65. Commit to a service ministry that helps those in need.
66. Commit to tutoring an inner-city student for an entire school year.
67. Visit a family from your community that lost a son or daughter in military action since 9/11 and thank them for their sacrifice.
68. Take your grandchildren to a Veterans Day parade and explain the meaning of the day to them.

69. Utilize some special skill you have to provide a lesson about American history at a local elementary school.
70. Memorize all stanzas of *America The Beautiful*.

Appendix II
Websites for Reference

With the proliferation of the internet age, the mass of the collective consciousness can be found online in a handy searchable form. The internet, while approached with skepticism, can provide any number of resources that illustrate every side of the debate concerning religion in America, Christianity, and the founding of our America, and Christians and their responsibilities in our country as patriots. Here are some of the websites that have been helpful to me over the past year.

The Constitution on the Web
The Constitution US website is one of the best I've found. It has the full Constitution and Bill of Rights. It has a helpful discussion of spelling, definitions, etc., with reference to the original documents. It is very good for high school and college students, especially as a resource: http:// constitutionus.com/.

Carry-Around Documents
This site offers a pocket-size version of the founding documents for $4.99, including shipping and handling. In addition, there are other good resources available here http://www.usconstitution.net/.

The Media and the Constitution
On January 6, 2011, the Republican-dominated House read the Constitution on the floor. For the flavor of the media response and the entire document go to this site:
http://www.huffingtonpost.com/2011/01/06/us-constitution-text-foun_n_805420.html.

Constitution and Citizenship Day
A little-known day of recognition is Constitution Day, celebrated September 17. This holiday has been in existence for over 100 years, and is the conflation of two holidays: Constitution Day and Citizenship Day. Resources for the celebration of Constitution and Citizenship Day are found throughout the web, but a good one for instruction and families is here: http://www.constitutioncenter.org/ncc_progs_Constitution_Day.aspx.

This site is also a great educational tool. Teachers and others can glean a great deal of knowledge here: http://www.loc.gov/law/help/commemorative-observations/constitution-day.php.

The Heritage Foundation
A conservative policy research group almost a million strong in membership. http://www.heritage.org/.

Family Vacations in Colonial America
A Google search by "family tours of Colonial America" produced more than ten pages of options. This is both an opportunity and a recommendation that I wish someone would have persuaded me to follow when my family was young! Allow me to make this recommendation to you: plan a family vacation once a year that includes a tour of Colonial America sites and later historical sites. Plan a reading schedule and a monthly family meeting to prep the family to enjoy and benefit from the trip. It will be well worth it in the future!

Disney's Hall of the Presidents
Disney has produced a great show that educates, the Hall of the Presidents. It is worth a Disney vacation just to sit through this show—at least twice. http://disneyworld.disney.go.com/parks/magic-kingdom/attractions/hall-of-presidents/.

Appendix III
Affirmations and Denials

The Judeo-Christian ethical framework provided a culture in which personal and political freedom found stability. *A Call to Christian Patriotism* is not a call to persecute, demean, or isolate anyone from enjoying the pursuit of happiness. This is what is unique about biblical Christianity. It recognizes God as the Creator. It recognizes God as the provider of the ethical framework that makes all human relationships workable. Remember the story that Jesus told of the Good Samaritan. Here was a man who stopped along the road to help a religious and national enemy. He risks his own welfare. He interrupts his own schedule. He gets his hands dirty transporting the man to an inn. He spends his own money to ensure that the man receives food and care. He returns to check on him and pay any additional expenses.

Biblical Christianity and the American *experiment* lives life in this manner. It means that the best neighbor a Muslim can have is an American who lives by this ethical framework. It means that the best friend an atheist can have is an American who lives by this ethical framework. It means that the best mayor a city can have is an American that lives by this ethical framework. This Judeo-Christian ethical framework has produced the greatest nation in the history of the world. Has it been perfect? NO! This is why we have courts. This is why we have both civil and criminal law. But, the general tenor of life benefitting the greatest number for the greatest amount of time has been the product of this ethic that is embedded in the foundational documents of America.

This book is not about demanding that all Americans become evangelical religious participants. But this book is about:

1) Calling all Christians regardless of denominational affiliation to evangelism (making a clear offer of the salvation provided through the life, death and resurrection of Jesus Christ) and discipleship (teaching believers to live a Christian life under the Lordship of Jesus Christ).

2) Calling all Christians to live their personal lives in a manner that glorifies God at all times

3) Calling all Christians to revitalization of the church in obedience to Christ (which is ultimately the only hope of revitalizing the nation)

4) Calling all Christians to intellectually defend the Judeo-Christian framework as the foundation of the American culture which invites people of any ethnic, religious, or cultural origin to embrace it— thus becoming part of this American culture known as the *melting pot*

5) Calling all Christians to personal and corporate repentance for not engaging in our civic responsibilities and thereby contributing to America veering from the framework provided by God through our Founding Fathers

6) Calling all Christians to engage in *rebuilding the walls* (to draw on the historical work of Nehemiah in the Old Testament) through active participation in the public square. We must expect opposition as did Nehemiah. We must not be intimidated as Nehemiah was not derailed by name calling and threats.

7) Calling all Christians to rejoice in God's *good hand* upon us and pray for God's sustaining and reviving grace through the teaching of the Word of God.

One other qualifier should be noted. This book is not about promoting Dominionism, Theonomy, or Reconstructionism. It is not an appeal for, or suggestion that, only Christians should occupy positions of power in American society. It is saying, however, that Christians should examine the lives of potential leaders in terms of their understanding and commitment to the Judeo-Christian ethical framework embedded in the founding documents. It is saying that Christians should seek to convince the public of the necessity to use this grid in their determining for whom they vote. It is saying that Christians should not be—in fact cannot be—intimidated by those who would bully them by name calling and misrepresentation while calling for a new form of government.

About the Author

Dr. Eyrich has earned four graduate degrees since completing a BA degree from Bob Jones University: the MDiv from Faith Theological Seminary, the ThM from Dallas Theological Seminary, the MA from Liberty University, and the DMin from Western Seminary. He also earned a Certificate in Gerontology from the University of Georgia and is ABD in psychology from California Coast University.

In his fifty-year career, he has served as a church planter, a senior pastor, a college professor, a seminary professor, and a seminary president. He currently serves as the Pastor of Counseling at Briarwood Presbyterian Church in Birmingham, Alabama.

He is married to Pamela Clark Eyrich, and they have two children. Tammy is married to a PCA pastor, and they have five children. David is a landscape architect and has three children.